I AM BACK

How A Soul Reincarnates

Bruce Robert Travis

"And if I go and prepare a place for you, I will come again."

© Photograph: Brian Lockett

The Orion Constellation and its spiritual significance for mankind is to be found in Job 38:31-33

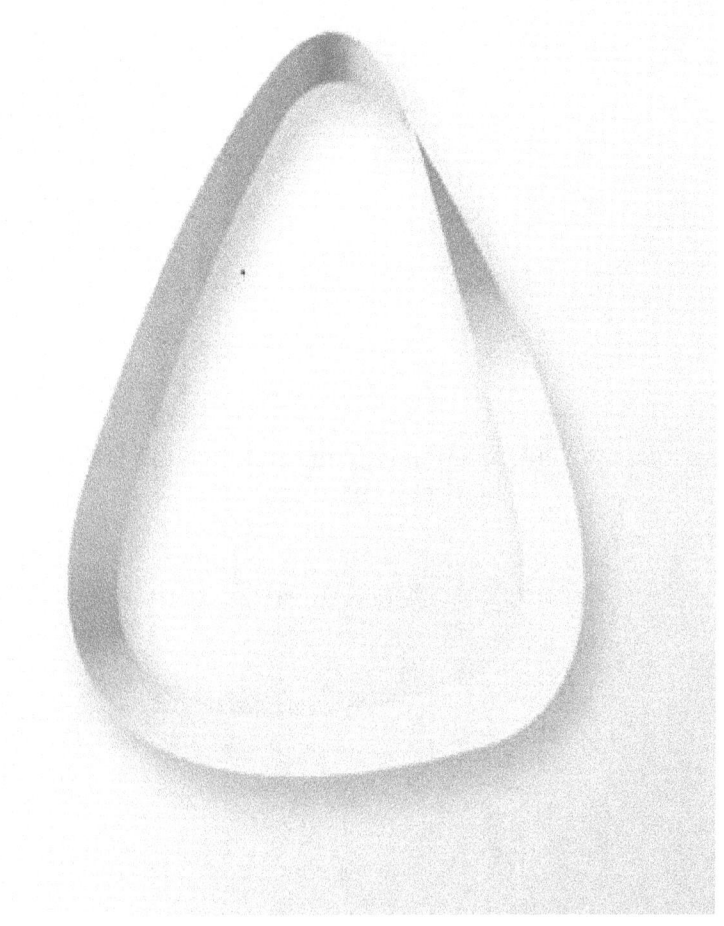

A human being living in the third dimensional world of duality and illusion is like the Mobius strip; one sided with only one boundary existing in 3D space. When we re-member and re-create who we truly are, we enter as soul beings, into higher states of consciousness and become multi-dimensional, limitless, with no boundaries.

A model can easily be created by taking a paper strip and giving it a half-twist, and then joining the ends of the strip together to form a loop.

Consider an object with one side and one edge existing in 3D space -what might a 5th, 6th or 7th dimensional object look like to us, observing as we do in 3 dimensional space?

"Condemnation without investigation is the highest form of ignorance."

Albert Einstein

"Let the world know why you are here, and do it with passion."

Wayne Dyer

1940-2015

"One man cannot change the world, but
one man can communicate the message that
will change the world"

Betty Shine

Acknowledgments

I would like to thank the following:

God for His/Her Intelligent Design for Creation

My wife Elise for her patience

My daughter … for her love

My mother and father for their unconditional love

Charles Hasbrook for his longtime friendship and brilliant insights

John Philpin for his support, knowledge and just 'being there'

To Cynthia Conrad and her dramatic cover designs for *I AM BACK-How A Soul Reincarnates.*

To Rikki Guy for his amazing 3D image of the Mobius strip.

Publishing Information

ISBN: 978-0-9846731-2-4

WARNING AND DISCLAIMER

This book is designed to provide information in regard to the subject matter covered. Every effort has been made to make it as complete and as accurate as possible. However, there may be mistakes (to err is human), both typographical and in content. Therefore, this book should be used only as a general guide and as a reflection of your own true self.

Contents

Contents viii

Preface ix

   Prologue - Re-entry xiii
   Decoding The Prologue xvi
   Letter To Shirley MacLaine xx
   There Shall Be Signs In The Heavens xxv
   Soul Readings From The Chinese Book Of Oracle I Ching xxviii

Part One 1

   1: The Times They Are A-Changin' 2
   2: Master It Or It Will Master You 9
   3: The Signs [1974] 18
   4: First Miracles? 26
   5: Numbers of Destiny 35
   6: The Law of Attraction Really Works 43
   7: The Two Marriages 49
   8: The Ernest Digweed Estate, Halloween, The Worst Winter 64
   9: Telling The Story [1978 to 1981] 73
   10: MY Fate is Sealed [1982 to 1984] 84

Part Two 93

   11: It is all based on cause and effect 94
   12: Pattern Identity = Person Identity 101
   13: The Seal Of Approval 113
   14: The Messianic Composite 121
   15: The Makings of a Messiah 133
   16: It's All About Personality 138
   17: Creation, Jacob's Ladder, Hu-Man 145
   Appendix 1: Book References 170
   Pope Arrested For Believing In Reincarnation 172
   Epilogue 173

Preface

If you are one of the 87 million Americans and 25% of the 1.18 billion Catholics in the world that believe in reincarnation then *I Am Back-How A Soul Reincarnates* will give you a deeper insight into the process of how a soul reincarnates lifetime after lifetime in a very concise scientific and metaphysical parameter.

Bruce's goal is to take you to a deeper level of reality and conscious awareness where you know that you are the reincarnation of you, the eternal and ever-lasting you that has lived many, many lifetimes before.

Two thousand years ago Jesus did say as recorded in *John 14:3* "I will come again" and he declared publicly exactly when he would 'come again.' Bruce's process, journey and quest into his own self-discovery he is willing to share with you.

The past is past but it has all been recorded and frozen in time. The purpose of *I Am Back-How A Soul Reincarnates* is to demonstrate the process of the reincarnating soul's journey, lifetime after lifetime, defining how our personalities, character traits, individuality, habits, patterns and even our body and facial architecture remain nearly identical. We are here to re-member and re-create who we are. If we do not do this in this lifetime, i.e. re-create ourselves as who we really are we cannot be who we truly are.

Just as the fourteenth Dali Lama is the reincarnation of his predecessor, the thirteenth Dali Lama, the fourteenth Dali Lama's soul is the same one that inhabited the body of the thirteenth. "The body changes but the soul remains the same." The old flesh body of Jesus from 2,000 years ago is not coming back ever. What you get with Bruce is the same soul that inhabited the body of Jesus but in a new similar-looking, but different, body. As will be demonstrated to you in great detail, the personality of Jesus is an exact match to Bruce's present life personality. Using his life as an example you will be the judge and jury in the examination of the hard evidence presented and render a verdict if you are the reincarnation of you.

Our planet and its humanity is in deep trouble in all ways and is suffering. The good news is that the pervasive negativity and division amongst its peoples can be turned positive and unified. It is all about raising consciousness and it will take a united spiritual effort on a global level to make the needed consciousness changes.

Humanity is being given the opportunity to exercise its interconnected One-ness now.

A book of poetry entitled *Messiah For Hire-Poems From Inner Space 1966-1982* is being released simultaneously with *I Am Back-How A Soul Reincarnates*. The poetry chronicles Bruce's spiritual awakening and parallels the biographical section in the opening chapters of *I Am Back-How A Soul Reincarnates*.

For meta-physicians and astrologers or anyone who might be interested Bruce has written a book called *The Horoscope of Jesus-The Spiritual Anatomy of a Messiah* and is a comparative analysis of the past life and present life horoscopes of Jesus and Bruce.

For psychologists, psychiatrists, therapists and psychoanalysts he has written a book centered around the Forensic Psychological Evaluations (of him) by Dr. Marvin B. Acklin PhD (for the defense) and Dr. Harold V. Hall PhD (for the prosecution). Two psychiatrists (one Board Certified) have given him a perfectly clean bill of mental health. Upon his release from federal prison he was also given a clean mental bill of health by two clinical psychologists paid for by the Federal Government. Rule out crazy and delusional.

If the information in this book helps you in any way into the discovery of who you really are, which is the soul's goal, then he will have succeeded in fulfilling his mission, destiny and higher purpose.

When Oprah Winfrey introduced Eckhart Tolle to the world in 2008 she implored her audience 'to keep an open mind.' This will be your challenge as well when reading this book.

Staying grounded and humble for him is easy knowing who the boss is.

"Wisdom is knowing how little we know." -

Socrates, 469 to 399 BCE

Prologue - Re-entry

Easter Sunday fell on the twenty-eighth day of March in 1948. It was now April second and the winds of the Ides of March were still howling outside and batting the branches of the budding maple and elm trees against the windows of room 343 of the Lying Inn Hospital at the University of Chicago* in the other Hyde Park.

The city itself incorporated in 1837 and in 1891 the University followed suit. On this day, the second of April, the planet Jupiter was in the twenty-eighth degree of the Scorpio constellation (In the sidereal system of Astrology) and Venus, the planet symbolizing love was in the twenty-eighth degree of the Aries constellation in exact conjunction to the fixed star *Alcyone*, the star known in ancient cultures as the Foundation Stone, the Central One and the brightest star in the Pleiades open cluster. It is believed that our sun and solar system revolves around *Alcyone*.

There were still small patches of sooty black snow on the ground and the light rain was doing its best to wash away the grime from the still salted streets. It was chilly cold outside, not quite freezing, but the wind could cut to the bone and the solid grey skies added to the gloom of another dreary, overcast early spring day in Chicago.

Rosamond, born in Cleveland, Ohio, was twenty-six years old when she gave birth to her second son Bruce Robert, named after the Scottish King *Robert the Bruce* who defeated the English at the battle of Bannockburn in 1314. Rosamond's father Benjamin, named after one of the Jewish tribes, was also born in the same year that the University of Chicago incorporated; 1891.

Louis, Bruce's father was born in Chicago, Illinois on January 17, 1918, and could not be there for the birth. He had an automobile detailing business and was working hard to make sure he could provide for the extra mouth to feed. Rosamond had to literally beg Louis to have another child because initially he was opposed to the idea but after relentless persistence Rosamond prevailed and Louis changed his mind and welcomed the future addition to the family 'clan.'

It wasn't an especially prolonged labor and at precisely 8:38 a.m. unbeknownst to the unsuspecting parents but according to a very well thought out master plan and intelligent design, Jesus reincarnated to the third dimensional reality and correctional facility known as planet earth...again!

The delivery room lights, noise, chatter and bustle of activity were quite a shocking change for me when I abruptly exited from the serenity, inner peace and security of my mother's womb's inner sanctum. As with all returning souls, the memory of *My Past Life as Jesu*s was stored safely deep in my subconscious mind at the moment of birth. Those past life memories would begin percolating to the surface in the 1960's and then those memories would become fully activated in 1973 when I awakened from the dream of the material illusion and remembered my past life identity as Y'shua; Aka Jesus.

My re-entry, rebirth if you will, went smoothly and after nearly two thousand years earth time but only five and one half years 'other side' time *(Ezekiel 4:6,7* one year for one day), I was back as promised *(John 14:1-3)* to complete my mission, fulfill my destiny, and accomplish my higher spiritual purpose. As owner of birth certificate number 430687 I had returned to earth to make my spiritual mark upon the world, and to empower humanity with the power of love.

As Jesus predicted to happen, exactly forty-two days after he reincarnated, his prophecy in *Matthew 24:32,* came to be fulfilled with the re-birth of the nation of Israel on May 14, 1948. The 'fig tree' had sprouted its leaves and Jesus was now at the world's door about to enter. The generation born when Israel was born would still be alive in 2015.

* Chicago is a city in the United States of America.

Decoding The Prologue

'Easter Sunday fell on the...' Sunday is the first day of the week. It is day # **1**.

In 1948 Easter was on the twenty-eighth day **(28)**. 2+8=**10**. 1+0=**1.**

'It is now April 2nd'. April is the 4th month. Add the 4th month to the 2nd day to the year 1948. 4+2+1+9+4+8=**28**. 2+8=**10**. 1+0=**1**.

'against the windows of room 343.' 3+4+3= 73. 7+3= **10**. 1+0=**1**

'At the University of Chicago.' Pythagoras in the sixth century BCE devised a system that measured things and names in terms of vibrations. In order to determine the vibration of a name or a thing he ascribed a number for each letter of the alphabet. Since numbers can only go from one to nine before they reduce to the lowest common denominator the system looked like this

1	2	3	4	5	6	7	8	9
A	B	C	D	E	F	G	H	I
J	K	L	M	N	O	P	Q	R
	S	T	U	V	W	X	Y	Z

3	8	9	3	1	7	6
C	H	I	C	A	G	O

3+8+9+3+1+7+6=37. 3+7=**10** and 1+0=**1**

'The city itself incorporated in 1837.'
1+8+3+7=19 and 1+9=**10** and 1+0= **1**.

'And in 1891 the University followed suit.'
1+8+9+1= 19 and 1+9=**10** and 1+ 0=**1**

'The planet Jupiter was in the twenty-eighth degree **(28)** of the Scorpio constellation.' (All placements are sidereal.)
28 degrees. 2+8=**10** and 1+0=**1**.

'And Venus, the planet of love was in the twenty-eighth **(28)** degree of Aries.
2+8=**10** and 1+0=**1**.

'Venus was exactly conjunct the fixed star Alcyone.' Alcyone is at twenty-eight degrees **(28)** of the Aries constellation.
2+8=**10** and 1+0=**1**.

'Rosamond's father Benjamin...born in 1891.'
1+8+9+1=19 and 1+9=**10** and 1+0=**1**.

'Louis Travis, Bruce's father, was born...on January 17, 1918...'
1+1+7+1+9+1+8=**28** and 2+8=**10** and 1+0=**1**.

'And at precisely 8:38 A.M....'
8+3+8=19 and 1+9=**10** and 1+0=**1**.

'The owner of birth certificate number 430687 had...'
4+3+0+6+8+7=**28** and 2+8=**10** and 1+0=**1**.

When I turned sixteen years old, I was issued a social security number that adds up to a number twenty-eight. XXX-XX-XXXX= **28**. 2+8=**10**. 1+0=**1**.

*"Chicago is a city in the UNITED States of America." UNITED = **28**. 2+8=**10**. 1+0=**1**.

The number twenty-eight, nineteen and other numbers adding up to the number ten (10), appear throughout my life in such amazing synchronicity that it defies statistical probability.

Physicist Paul Davies in *The Mind of God* (1992, pp.213-215) said: "The natural world is not just any old concoction of entities and forces, but a marvelously ingenious and **unified mathematical scheme.** Each new discovery is a clue which finds its solution in some new mathematical linkage and one begins to see a pattern emerge. To what purpose has God produced this design? The universe looks as if it is unfolding according to some **plan** or **blueprint**, the product of intelligent design."

These are the words of a physicist and are the basis, framework and guide for this book which reveals the following: There exists a...

"Unified mathematical scheme and…

Each new discovery is a clue, which finds its solution in…

Some new mathematical linkage and…

One begins to see a pattern emerge.

To what purpose has God produced this design? It is unfolding according to…

Some plan or blueprint.

The product of intelligent design."

The Jewish mystical Qabalah(to receive wisdom) teaches that the "soul is measured at birth" and that the birth numbers reveal the state of the soul and is a measure of its spiritual alignment in relation to God. Modern mathematical physics retains the ancient Greek assumption that the universe is rationally ordered according to mathematical principles. This mathematical order has to do with the coded number **28.** Pythagoras was convinced the cosmic order was based on numerical relationships and that number was the measure of all things and that the perfect numbers were 6 and **28**, with greatest respect for the number **10** which reduces to **1.**

Letter To Shirley MacLaine

Shirley MacLaine

Atria Books/Simon & Schuster

1230 Avenue of the Americas

New York, New York 10020

Re: Correction to Page 99 of I'm Over All That

Dear Shirley,
2011

Thank you for sharing your journey with us. On May 22, 1993, I was given a copy of Out On A Limb. Reading it further validated my own experience of reincarnation and my own 'quest for myself.' Twenty years before, in 1973, I received confirmation of a past life, which I have been documenting ever since on scientific and metaphysical levels. You would think that, after 38 years, I would be 'over' this verification process, but I am driven by the words of Dr. Ian Stevenson who is looking for 'that one case' that will prove to the world that reincarnation exists. The global acceptance of reincarnation will transform the planet and bring about the 'Brotherhood of Man.' Idealistic thinking, for sure, but I believe it is coming and coming soon.

On page 99 of I'm Over All That, I think you may have misread the quote in Matthew 16:13-14 *about who Jesus thought he had been in a past life. It was the disciples, and not Jesus, who were confused as to who he was. Jesus did not 'allude to the truth that he had been Elias or Elijah previously' or that he was 'Jeremias, John the Baptist or one of the prophets.' (13) 'When Jesus came into the coasts of Caesarea Philippi, he asked his disciples, saying, "Whom do men say that I, the Son of Man, am?" (14) and they said, "Some say that thou art John the Baptist; some, Elias; and others, Jeremias, or one of the prophets..." The mystery is cleared up in Matthew 11:7-15 and Matthew 17:10-13, when Jesus teaches the disciples that John was the reincarnation of Elijah/Elias and the disciples 'understood' this. 17:13.*

In Revelation 5:5, it is intimated that maybe Jesus was King David (in a prior lifetime) and in Revelation 22:16, Jesus 'alludes' to whom he may have been in one of his prior incarnations: "I am the root and the offspring of David." This is merely speculation and we do not know for sure how many references to reincarnation which have been edited out of the Gospels (at the Council of Nicea in 325 A.D. and in 553 A.D. by Empress Theodora of Byzantium) would give us more clues as to who was whom and when.

What we do know for sure and what the world is completely missing (it's so obvious) is that Jesus, a mystic and initiate, predicted his own reincarnation in John 14:3, "I will come again and receive you unto myself" and he even told us exactly when he would reincarnate.

In Matthew 24:3, the disciples, knowing this, asked a simple question of him: "What shall be the sign of thy coming and the end of the world?" Jesus gives them all kinds of 'signs' to look for, but the one that pinpointed exactly when he would reincarnate was in Matthew 24:32-34. The 'fig tree,' as historians know, symbolizes the nation of Israel. So, Jesus answers their question of what the 'sign' is that he has reincarnated. Israel was reborn on May 14, 1948, 'coincidentally' the same year that world-renowned meta physician, Alice A. Bailey, released her book, The Reappearance of the Christ. *So, Jesus reincarnated just prior to the rebirth of the nation of Israel, just as he predicted.*

The next major clue comes in verse 34, when he discloses when he will make his 'reappearance' on the world's stage and he gives the exact time for that event, i.e. 'This generation shall not pass.'

First clue: How many years in a generation? The Greek historian Herodotus learned from the Pharaoh's of Egypt that there were three Pharaoh kings to a generation, or every 33.3 years.

Second clue: The 'end of the world' in Matthew 24:3 really means 'the end of the age' (of Pisces) and that is where all the 'rapture' and 'end of the world' nonsense arises (Harold Camping and that ilk).

Third Clue: In Mark 14:13, Jesus tells the disciples how to find the place where the Passover dinner ('Last Supper') is being secretly held. 'Go into the city and there you will meet a man bearing a pitcher of water: follow him.' Is it merely 'coincidence' that the astrological sign of Aquarius is represented by a person 'bearing a pitcher of water' and that this clue coincided with the Passover dinner? Jesus is telling us that the precessional sun will have 'passed over' from Pisces to Aquarius and that the generation born when Israel was born will still be alive to witness his 'reappearance' event, i.e. 'receive you unto myself.'

The precessional sun 'passed over' from Pisces to Aquarius on January 26, 2008 when the planet Pluto entered the sign Sagittarius (in the sidereal system) 'marking a period of spiritual regeneration at the beginning of the Aquarian age...' 1

1. The Astrologer's Handbook by Sakoian & Acker 1973 p.227.

The greatest of 'fundamental laws' is the law of cause and effect (karma and reincarnation).

Thank you for taking the time to read my letter.

Joy, truth and love.

Sincerely,

Bruce Robert Travis

There Shall Be Signs In The Heavens

2000 years ago in the New Testament Book of *John 14:2,3* Jesus said: *"I go to prepare a place for you. And if I go and prepare a place for you I WILL COME AGAIN and receive you unto myself..."* Has humanity ever considered the possibility that Jesus was speaking about his own reincarnation? In *Matthew 24:32-36* Jesus predicted he would be reborn when the ancient nation of Israel was reborn in 1948 and even predicted when he would make his presence on Earth known in 2015 but not to the "day or hour." He gave all the clues to his "coming." *"Those who have an ear will hear!"*

In *Matthew 24:3* the disciples ask Jesus: "What shall be the sign of thy coming...?" In *Luke 21:25* Jesus tells them. *"... there shall be SIGNS in the sun, and in the moon and in the stars..."* In the Shemitah year of 1987 a supernova could be seen by the naked eye for the first time since 1604. *Genesis 1:14*. "And God said: let there be lights in the firmament of the heaven to divide the day from the night; and let them be for *SIGNS* and for seasons." A "season" is an appointed time. The appointed time is a "set time" (*Psalms 102:13*) and represents the reappearance on the world stage of the soul of Jesus in the physical body of Bruce.

800 years before the birth of Jesus, *Joel* in *2:30,31* said: "I will show wonders in the heavens and in the earth, blood and fire, and pillars of smoke. The sun shall be turned into darkness and the moon into blood before the great and the terrible day of the Lord come." In *Luke 21:19,20* Jesus quoting Joel says *"I will show wonders in the heaven above and signs in the earth beneath; blood*

and fire, and vapor of smoke. The sun shall be turned into darkness, and the moon into blood, before that great and notable day of the Lord come." Psalms 19: 1 *"The heavens declare the glory of God."* Revelation 6:12 *"...the sun became black...and the moon became as blood."*

WHAT ARE THESE "WONDERS" IN THE HEAVENS?

According to the National Aeronautics and Space Administration (NASA) there have been several Tetrads of four consecutive blood moons since the agency first recorded their occurrences. Tetrads coinciding with major Jewish historical events have only occurred three times in the past 500 years and have occurred on Jewish high holy days. What will be the historical event for the final Tetrad blood moon cycle of 2014-2015?

The first series of Tetrad blood moons occurred from Passover April 2* 1493 following the expulsion of the Jews from Spain to Sukkot on September 15,1494.

The 2nd series of Tetrad blood moons came following the re-birth of Israel on May 14, 1948* from Passover April 13, 1949 to Sukkot on September 26, 1950.

The 3rd Tetrad of blood moons came during the time of the Six Day War in Israel from Passover April 24, 1967 to Sukkot October 6, 1968.

And now the culmination of the 4th Tetrad blood moon cycle that began on Passover April 15, 2014 ("the moon became as blood") then a total solar eclipse("the sun became black") on March 20, 2015, then the next blood moon on Passover April 4, 2015 with the final Tetrad perigee "super" blood moon on Sukkot September **28**, 2015. This is it! The next Tetrad of blood moons will not occur until 2031-2033 and the generation born when Israel became a nation will have passed.

Unlike the other three Tetrads the final Tetrad of 2014-2015 is in the midst of a Shemitah year (seven year cycle) that began on Rosh Hashanah September 25, 2014 ending on the eve of Rosh Hashanah September 13, 2015, the 29th of Elul and my daughter's **28**th birthday.. Shemitah means "**release.**" Is something big going to be released to create an historical event for Israel? At 12:00 midnight on September **28,** 2015 when the "super" blood moon was at 15 degrees Pisces (sidereal) in conjunction with my natal Sun 12 degrees 46 minutes of Pisces (sidereal) *I AM BACK-HOW A SOUL REINCARNATES* was *released* to the world; that is, the book was born and became a published work.

* I was reborn on April 2, 1948. Two blood moons occurred on my birthday of April 2nd. One of them on Passover 1950.

"During the last half of September there is a powerful wave of gamma light coming from the galactic core. This intergalactic wave X energy will be coming through to earth through maximum strength and peaking on the fourth and final super blood moon on September **28**, 2015. We are already well into it and feeling its effects. It happens every 3,600 years and is called the Event Horizon. **It is the next step in the evolutionary cycle of man.** As reported in Time Magazine scientists know about this event but question what the mysterious intergalactic bursts are or more importantly what they will bring. **Change for sure.** It is no coincidence that earthquakes have quadrupled in the last 18 months as this energy is being felt more and more on the planet.

This is a time when our cellular DNA is able to shift and open up our true gifts." Dr. Kathy Forti - *Fractals of God.*

Credit and copyright to Johannes Schedler

Soul Readings From The Chinese Book Of Oracle I Ching

MAY 26, 2015 TO SEPTEMBER 1, 2015

I have been keeping a record of my soul readings since 1969 when my brother Craig gave me a copy of the I Ching on May 1, 1969. I have been acutely aware of my mission on Earth since 1973. The final Tetrad blood moon cycle of 2014-2015 was an indicator that the time of my reappearance was approaching. The following is an overview of the three readings since May 2015. The I Ching is a measurement of the soul's energetic vibration tied to synchronicity and is a psychic event. Like prayer, it is hard to define exactly how the universe knows and measures the soul's intentions, but it knows.

May 26, 2015 - On this date I drew hexagram #49 called Revolution/Molting with 9 in the 1st place and 9 in the 3rd place. "The moltings of political life, the great revolutions connected with changes of government. The Judgment. Revolution. On your day you are believed. Supreme success. Furthering through perseverance. Remorse disappears. One brings about a revolution (spiritual) and in doing so is trusted. Enlightenment, and thereby joyousness. You create great success through justice. If in a revolution one hits upon the right thing, "remorse disappears." Heaven and earth bring about revolution and the four seasons complete themselves thereby. Political revolution comes about by being submissive toward heaven and in accord with men. The time of revolution is truly great.

The changing lines in the first hexagram created the follow up hexagram # 45, Gathering Together/Massing which in its essence means "only collective moral force can unite the world."

August 2, 2015- On this date I drew hexagram # 46 called "Pushing Upward" with 6 in the 4th place which means "Direct rise from obscurity and lowliness to power and influence. Pushing upward has supreme success. One must see the great man. Fear not. Departure toward the south brings good fortune. The yielding pushes upward with the time. Gentle and devoted. The firm is in the middle and finds correspondence, hence it attains great success. One must see the great man. Fear not for it brings blessing. Departure toward the south brings good fortune. What is willed is done. To achieve great success it is said one must see the great man. The reason for success is not an earthly but a transcendental one. The favorableness of the conditions comes from the invisible world. This hexagram indicates a stage in which pushing upward attains its goal. One acquires fame in the sight of Gods and men, is received into the circle of those who foster the spiritual life of the nation, and thereby attains a significance that endures beyond time.

The changing line in the first hexagram created the follow up hexagram # 32 of Duration, which in its essence means "a state whose movement is not worn down by hindrances. Duration is the self-contained and self-renewing movement of an organized, firmly integrated whole, taking place in accordance with immutable laws and beginning anew at every ending so likewise the dedicated man embodies an enduring meaning in his way of life, and thereby the world is formed."

September 1, 2015 - On this date I drew hexagram # 34 called "Power of the Great" with 9 in the 2nd place. Perseverance furthers. This hexagram points to a time when inner worth mounts with great force and comes to power. But its strength has already passed beyond the median line, hence there is danger that one may rely entirely on one's own power and forget to ask what is right. There is danger too that, being intent on movement, we may not wait for the right time. Therefore the added statement that perseverance furthers. For that is truly great power, which does not degenerate into mere force but remains inwardly united with the fundamental principles of right and justice. When we understand this point- namely, that greatness and justice must be indissolubly united-we understand the true meaning of all that happens in heaven and on earth. Thus the superior man does not tread upon paths that do not accord with established order. True greatness depends on being in harmony with what is right. Therefore in times of great power the superior man avoids doing anything that is not in harmony with the established order. 9 in the 2nd place means "the gates to success are beginning to open. Resistance gives way and we forge ahead. Perseverance in inner equilibrium, without excessive use of power brings good fortune."

The changing line in the first hexagram created the follow up hexagram # 55 called Abundance [Fullness] which in its essence means: "It is not given to every mortal being to bring about a time of outstanding greatness and abundance. Only a born ruler of men is able to do it, because his will is directed to what is great... He must be like the sun at midday, illuminating and gladdening everything under heaven." *

*The I Ching or Book of Changes by Wilhelm/Baynes. 1969 edition.

"The task is...not so much to see what no one has yet seen, but to think what nobody has yet thought, about that which everybody sees."

Physicist Erwin Schrodinger

Part One

1: The Times They Are A-Changin'

I was twenty-five years old in 1973, when God confirmed my intuitive belief that the soul of Jesus was inside me enveloping my physical and spiritual body. That was the year I had my 'religious experience' except I wasn't religious at the time. It was my spiritual re-awakening and resurrection from being asleep and unconscious to my past life identity as Jesus.

Even though I am Jewish by the blood of my mother and father, my grandparents and my ancestors, I was not raised in the Jewish tradition and faith. I knew nothing of Torah or why a Jew was a Jew and I understood even less about Jesus, except that I knew deep inside that I had been Jesus in a previous lifetime. God had given me a sign, encouraged me to 'knock on the door' and assured me that the door would open. God spoke to me the following words: "Master it or it will master you." But, we are getting ahead of the story, which really began years before.

My journey into the mystical realm began in 1969 when I married my first wife, Carol. My older brother, Craig, gave me a copy of the *I Ching, Chinese Book of Oracle* as a wedding present which gave me a new perspective into the nature of reality. It awakened in me an awareness that a higher power knew exactly what was going on in my life when I wasn't quite so sure.

The day after we were married, on May 1st, Carol and I opened a 'Head Shop' called *The Headquarters, An Exquisite Freaque Boutique,* on Chicago's near north side. It was the wrong neighborhood to be in for such a business and within two months we had to close our doors. The police hassle just wasn't worth it.

My parents owned a real estate company and my father convinced me to use my gift for selling and to get my real estate license which I did on August 10th that year and so my professional career began at the tender age of twenty-one. My mom and dad showed me the proverbial 'ropes' and before long I was listing properties and selling up a storm. I quickly became one of the top producers in the company.

My brother Craig and I were brought up as Unitarians and attended the Beverly Unitarian Church at 103rd and Longwood Drive in

Beverly Hills, Chicago. The church was an actual reproduction of a European castle and even the large blocks of stone that were used for construction were authentic. Unitarianism isn't a religion. The people who become Unitarians tend to be fairly liberal with no particular mindset about God or the historically famous persons attached to those religions like Buddha, Krishna, Muhammad or Jesus. Unitarians believe what they want to believe so I grew up first as an atheist, like my parents, and then became agnostic, some time along the way. My parents gave us the choice to believe what we wanted to believe. The church had a Sunday school so there was no shortage of learning about the religions of the world and basic spiritual concepts. I had a very open mind and I was always eager to learn new things about life.

It was the mystical *I Ching,* however, that started me on the spiritual path that led to the discovery of who I had been in a past life. It made me more aware of the higher power, the universe, and gave me a greater self-awareness and higher consciousness. The sixty-four hexagrams of the *I Ching* was a study in mystical psychology. Now that my spiritual appetite had been whetted I was drawn to the other Chinese mystics like Confucius and Lao Tzu who authored the *Tao Te Ching* or *The Way.* Tao means how; i.e. how things happen in life and how things in the universe work. I learned early on that Tao is a principal and creation is a process. This was my foundation to build upon and I was ready.

At the age of fourteen, I started high school at the Clissold branch of Morgan Park High School. That was in 1962. Our family moved out of that school district and into Evergreen Park, Illinois where I attended the community high school. In 1964 the Beatles came on the scene. Having learned how to play basic guitar in Mexico at the age of ten, I took guitar lessons when I returned home, bought my first electric guitar, found a drummer and a base player and formed my first band called *The Scarabs,* a kind of beetle. We wore grey 'Beatle' collarless suits, Beatle boots and I let my hair grow and wore it like The Beatles.

We played local parties and High School dances. I was the only one in the school with long hair. Anything compared to a crew cut was considered "long."

The word got around that the new kid was different from everybody else and before long I was called into the principal's office and was told to cut my hair or don't come back to school. I didn't cut my hair and my father paid the principal a visit and read him the 'riot act,' telling him, in no uncertain terms, that he could not curtail his son's right to freedom of expression. My dad always fought for my rights. He was a man ahead of his time when it came to human rights.

After graduating from Evergreen Park H.S. in 1965, my mom, dad, and I went and toured several colleges in Wisconsin and Illinois settling on Rockford College in Rockford, Illinois. The student population of fewer than three hundred lived on campus. I decided on English as a major but also took classes in philosophy and psychology along with history and drama. I took too many courses and struggled to keep up. I played the part of the young actor in the play *Six Characters In Search Of An Author* by Luigi Pirandello. Philosophy introduced me to Socrates, Plato, Aristotle and the other great thinkers of ancient Greece. Psychology 101 gave me more insight into the makeup of the human psyche, character, and the nature of personality and individuality in a psychological and psychodynamic framework.

My parents were avid readers, into classical music, opera, the arts, existentialism and avant-garde thought in general. But, it was Plato and Socrates who gave me my first taste of the concept of past lives and reincarnation, to which I was strongly attracted. I had already read many of my father's books by Jean Paul Sartre, Albert Camus and Jean Genet and my brother Craig, introduced me to the beat poets the likes of Alan Ginsberg, Kenneth Rexroth and comedians like Lenny Bruce and Tom Lehrer. My mind was open and ready.

By early 1966, I was was playing the songs of Bob Dylan, Donavon, Peter Paul and Mary, the Kingston Trio and dressing the part of a folk musician. I wore a Dylan Cap and boots and performed a concert at the college playing the harmonica while I played guitar and 'The Times They Were A-Changin.' That summer, I bought a 1956 red TR3 Triumph sports car from a college buddy for $300.00 and we drove to the *Newport Folk Festival* in Newport, Rhode Island. Pete Seeger, Joan Baez and other greats of the folk world were there. That was a fabulous experience. A real 'happening.'

Later that summer things changed dramatically. A near death in the family, my parents divorced and the times were in fact really changing. I decided to stay home with my dad and did not return to Rockford, College, attending instead the local junior college. I went to work on Wells Street in Old Town and sold men's high fashion clothing. I met Carol, bought a 1966 BMW R-60 motorcycle, played the coffee house circuit and started up a new band I called *The King James Version,* as in the *New Testament.*

Bogan Junior College was at 79th and Pulaski on Chicago's S.W. side, not far from Evergreen Park where my dad and I were living. It was in my anthropology class I discovered I had another gift and talent: research. I wrote a paper called *Man's Inhumanity To Man*, which I spent many happy hours researching. The teacher used my paper as a class example, reading it aloud, and even asked if she could keep it. Of course, I said, "yes!" I wish I had a copy.

That fall I received my first spiritual message in the guise of a poem; a transmission if you will. I didn't know it at the time but these poems were designed to stir up my consciousness and get me prepared for what was to come. The message spoke of peace, brotherhood, spiritual blindness and societal hypocrisy. It was an 'embryonic journey to my being' and not induced by any psychedelic drugs, which proliferated at that time. Timothy Leary and his LSD movement were big in Haight Ashbury in San Francisco and had made its way to the mid-west. People were 'tripping their brains out" on acid all over the place. Not me. I was working, going to college and playing music. I was on a natural high and things started accelerating.

It was six months after I had met Carol that I decided to call her. It was in February of 1967 when we began dating. I would drive my motorcycle in the snow all the way to Homewood/Flossmoor, which was a fair distance south away from 95th and Pulaski. I had roll bars in case I went down, which I did on a number of occasions. It was just plain crazy to drive a motorcycle in the winter but I fell in love with Carol and nothing could keep me away. I didn't have a car anymore.

That summer my dad bought a big old house at 98th and Longwood Dr. in Beverly Hills, Chicago, just a few blocks from the Unitarian Church. Carol moved in with me. My new band practiced in the basement and before long we began getting bookings and playing some of the top venues in the city. I met the other band members in Old Town and we were given permission to rehearse at the *Aardvark Theater* in *Piper's Alley*. Joe Zack was the lead player and he was great. He was into sitar music and could play Indian ragas on the guitar. *The King James Version* was what you would call an 'underground band.' We played Led Zeppelin, Jimmy Hendrix, Country Joe and The Fish, Pink Floyd, Jefferson Airplane and all the great 60's groups.

The *Second City* improvisational comedy club was right on Wells Street at the head of *Piper's Alley* and I often encountered the comedian, David Steinberg going to rehearsal. I became friends with Bernie Solens who was the owner of *Second City*, and I was right in there with the whole scene. It was December 1965 and the song '*Turn, Turn, Turn*' by The Byrds came out with verses from the Biblical book of *Ecclesiastics:* "To everything there is a season. A time for every purpose under heaven: A time to be born and a time to die, a time for war and a time for peace." What a great song. It really resonated with me.

The King James Version had become locally famous and we were the opening act for many of the big name bands that came to Chicago. I became friends with Jimmy Peterick of the band *The Ides Of March* who became famous with their song *Vehicle*. *The King James Version* opened for the *Ides of March* on many occasions and we recorded several original songs but they were never played on the radio.

In the summer of 1967 Carol and I were part of the 10,000 people strong peace march to Chicago's Civic Center in protest of the Vietnam war. Once at the Center, 'Chicago's finest,' as the police were called, stormed the crowd swinging their clubs and scattered the protestors. Carol and I made our way to *State Street,* which was nearby, and mixed in with the crowd. My hair was long; I wore striped bell-bottom pants and looked like a 'hippie.' The police weren't finished. They cordoned off one whole block of *State Street* and singled out anyone who did not look mainstream. One 'cop' began beating me on my head and wouldn't stop. Carol jumped on top of me to protect me and took a few hits herself. I was nearly unconscious and bleeding from my head profusely. Carol helped me up off the street and managed to flag a taxi to the nearest hospital, where the doctors stitched up a very battered skull.

A short time later, the police arrived at the Hospital and rounded up the marchers and took us to police headquarters at 12th and State where we were locked up. I had finally come to my senses and asked for the arresting officer, whom they could not produce, so Carol and I were released immediately.

I was draft age and notified to take the physical exam. I had 'pes planus' third degree (very flat feet), and luckily I was rejected for service to the very war that I was protesting. The Creator's plan did not call for my getting killed in Vietnam or killing another human being. The Vietnam War, like all other wars, was truly 'Man's Inhumanity To Man.'

In the summer of 1968, while the police beat up the protestors in Grant Park, *The King James Version* played for the reception of the Democratic Convention at the Conrad Hilton Hotel, with Mayor Daley hosting presidential hopeful, George McGovern.

In 1969, Carol and I were married by the Unitarian minister, I was introduced to the *I Ching and* passed the Illinois real estate salesman's exam. My parents remarried each other and remained so until my father's passing in October 2012.

2: Master It Or It Will Master You

Junior year was spent at Roosevelt University in downtown Chicago, the same school my father graduated from in 1955. English was still my major and I had the idea that I would become an English professor but the cosmic designer of the universe had other plans for me. In my English Renaissance class, I made a discovery and found a hidden meaning in a poem by John Skelton. My professor thought the paper was 'brilliant and ingenious' but gave me a C minus. I thought this was unfair and asked the pompous professor Bowersox to explain himself, to which he replied: 'we can't rewrite history.' I pleaded my cause to no avail. I went to my British literature professor for backup but received no support. I was being punished for my insightful observations. I became disenchanted with English and dropped out of both classes. I was an A student in English but received F's instead of giving in to this kind of fascist tactics. I completed my other classes and that was the end of my dream of being an English professor. This was not meant to be. It was a blessing in disguise.

It was now 1970, and after three years with Carol the relationship was beginning to unravel. I was growing spiritually, very loving and affectionate, but Carol was not reciprocating. We separated and then divorced in 1971. I re-organized my life, buried myself in work and passed the Illinois Broker's license exam. I convinced my parents to let me open a branch real estate office in Palos Hills, Illinois, where Carol and I had lived. I bought a house in Worth Woods, which was a few short blocks from the office and I began buying and selling properties.

I was doing quite well for myself and you could say that my material, carnal self was well in control. I was still reading the Chinese mystics and the poetic messages were still streaming through my consciousness but my focus was clearly on making money. I was honest, sincere, had integrity, and, all in all, I was a good person. I wasn't on the spiritual path yet but I was headed in the right direction.

Sometime in 1971, after my divorce, I met an angel. Not a literal angel, but a woman named Angel who helped me to open my heart even more to love. Her influence on me was profound. She loved me the way Carol couldn't and one day a poem came through my consciousness called *I Came Into The Universe* and my spirit began to quicken. Angel as it turned out, was a real Angel, and prepared me for my next big love.

I always wanted to own an Afghan hound. I found an ad in the paper for a litter and the owner lived in Old Town where I had worked years before. There must have been six or seven puppies, mostly a light sandy color, and one that was much lighter in color suddenly stopped playing with the others and came right over to me as if she knew I was coming to pick her up. I never bothered with the others; this was the one and she picked me. I named her Tashandi, Tasha for short, and we would be nearly inseparable for nearly fifteen years.

Real estate was going well. My father taught me how to appraise a property so each time I went on a listing appointment I gave the homeowner a free written appraisal from my Roy Wenzlick appraisal manual. This was not just a market analysis, but a real appraisal. The estimate of value was very accurate and it gave me a competitive edge over the other sales agents who were also trying to get the listing. I needed some type of advantage because I still kept my long hair and you just didn't see any of that on the southwest side of Chicago. Old Town, yes! North side, yes! Not the southwest side. I just wasn't willing to give up my individuality to sell real estate. I proved my professionalism and whatever I did, it worked.

On the biggest advertising days I would go directly to the *Southtown Economist Newspaper* and get the 'By Owner' ads hot off the press. I would be the first to call on the new listings and I signed up many exclusives, which is when the homeowner signed a contract with me to sell their house for a particular period of time. Some listings were so 'hot' that I would take a thirty-day listing and then sell it before the time was up. If the owner wouldn't sign an 'exclusive,' I asked for an 'open listing,' which meant that anybody could sell it. I sold many open listings. I had an uncanny ability to match the right buyer with the right house at the right time. I knew what my customers wanted and I would call them all excited to explain that I found their perfect house and most of the time I was right. It was amazing. I loved to sell real estate. Little did I know that this ability to match people to property was a trait I inherited from my past life as Jesus. In that past lifetime I was able to match each disciple with the proper prophecy to fulfill. Judas for example was the betrayer and Peter was the denier.

I was making really good money now, so I traded in my 1969 Chevrolet Impala for a new 1971 Mercury Brougham. The Palos Hills office was up and running and I expanded my reach into the southwest suburbs. Tasha was the love of my life now and I was happy. Life was fairly uncomplicated after four years of nothing but complications with Carol.

1971 came and went. In 1972, I met Karen, who became the next human love of my life. Karen was a graphic designer who lived on the far north side of Chicago, nearly an hour's drive away. Tasha and I would make the trip several times a week and it was worth it. Karen was beautiful, sexy and passionate but she did not want to be tied down so, after about a year and a half, when I wanted to get serious and she didn't, I ended the relationship.

I loved all the girls I dated, but some I loved more deeply than others and I made all of them feel special and loved. That was just the way I was and am.

Right before our relationship came to a grinding halt, I invited Karen to go to Maui with me, my parents and some friends of the family. While shopping on Front Street in Lahaina, we went into a *Crazy Shirts* shop and two shirts immediately caught my attention. One was a Superman shirt and the other was a sleeveless tank top in powder blue with a Jewish Star of David in a golden yellow with the Superman 'S' in the center of the star. Attached to the star were blue Angel wings and the mystical emblem looked like it was taking off. I bought both shirts immediately not knowing they were 'signs' from the Creator. These shirts would play a pivotal role in my destiny, as they were part of my awakening process. There can be no doubt I was drawn to those shirts...or, maybe the shirts drew me to them.

I was Jewish, looked like the historical portrayals of Jesus, and there in the *Crazy Shirt's* store was a Super Jew t-shirt. This did not register on a conscious level, but with my recent studies and with people calling me Jesus all the time, things were beginning to filter through into my conscious mind and slowly the connection to my past life as Jesus was being made.

There were other signs, too. This may sound strange to you but there are no coincidences in life. Things happen for a reason and a purpose just like the song '*Turn, Turn, Turn*' said. When my dad moved our family out of Marquette Park and into Beverly Hills, Chicago, in 1958, I attended the *Kate Starr Kellogg* grade school from fifth to eighth grade. Like *Rockford College,* the student population was tiny. There were only ten children in my graduating class. The majority of the neighborhood seemed to be Roman Catholic and directly across the street from Kellogg school was the *Christ The King* church and school with a gigantic stained glass window of Jesus himself. The catholic kids threw stones at the public school windows, but no one dared throw a stone at that imposing figure of Christ. Seeing that image every day must have been part of God's plan to begin waking me up, at such an early age, to my past life.

It seemed everyone said, 'Jesus Christ', 'for Christ's sake or Jesus H. Christ all the time. There was no getting away from Jesus. He was everywhere 'For Christ's sake.'

I had a passion for cars. With money flowing in, I could indulge.1972 was a particularly good year, so I leased a new *Lincoln Continental Mark IV* in brown just like the 1971 Mercury Brougham. I also bought a used red convertible 1963 XKE Jaguar roadster which was the beginning of my automobile nightmares. Materialism has a price. Between 1972 and 1974, I bought two XKE's, two Corvettes, one a 1963 tan split window coupe, an MGB roadster in red, another Mark IV and a Black Lincoln 1971 Mark III. It was almost a sickness. At one time, I had five cars sitting at my house. It was ridiculous, but it was part of the cosmic designer's plan. I had to reach a saturation point with being materially polluted. My cup was too full, too soon, and it needed to be empty before God could fully enter into my life. That is how spirituality works. One cannot be a slave to two masters. It is either one or the other. For me, it was still the 'other': money and material things. The secret to having both would be reached later.

In 1973 things started to change dramatically. I met Jim Dorchak, a brilliant musician and a student of metaphysics and mysticism. We quickly became friends and I invited Jim to move into my house with guitars, some clothes and books. Jim had a complete set of *The Secret Doctrine* by Madam Blavatsky, a famous 19th and early 20th century theosophist who founded the *Theosophical Society*. Members were versed in Qabala, the astral planes of the afterlife*, and all matters arcane and esoteric. Madam Blavatsky was a student of the gurus of India and she imparted all of her wisdom in *The Secret Doctrine*. During this time with Jim I studied her works and began reading books on astrology and UFO's. (* the before life)

With *The Secret Doctrine,* I learned more about reincarnation and that is when I connected the dots and had a strong suspicion that I was the reincarnation of Jesus. Jim and I would jam on guitar all night and discuss everything mystical. The books, *Seth Speaks* by Jane Roberts and *Be Here Now* by Baba Ram Das aka Richard Alpert were released that year. I was still selling real estate but my consciousness was shifting rapidly. Money was losing some of its importance; mystical studies became more dominant and life's events made more sense to me. *Christ The King Church*, *The King James Version* and the shirts from Maui the previous year. Why not? It felt right. I now understood the basics of the reincarnating soul, life after death, Qabala (to receive) and astrology. People had been calling me Jesus since at least 1967 and I was, after all, Jewish, just like Jesus. I was now ready for the next big step.

Before Jim came along, I had been taking baby steps towards spirituality. I had a good foundation with the Chinese mystics and the open mind of a Unitarian, so the ground was fertile for the planting. Jim affirmed my spirituality and I revealed to him my belief that I had been Jesus in a past life. At this very early stage in my (re) development, this past life belief was just a hunch, an inner knowing. I had come to a fork in the road. I had to make a choice. I could either continue putting all my energy into making money or I could pursue the unknown spiritual dimensions. The tangible for the intangible? The seen for the unseen? The known for the unknown?

I was not thinking about which path to take on a conscious level because I wasn't prepared yet to make that decision on my own. I was still much too entrenched in the material world and addicted to its rewards, but I was definitely going through material withdrawal. Jim was helping me to break the materialism 'habit.' Yes! Habitual, and a hard habit to break.

By autumn of 1973, the stage was set for my spiritual transformation and the experience that would change my life forever. My hair was really long now so I made an appointment with Bobbi, my hair stylist, to trim it up just a little. Bobbi was like a therapist and I always shared everything with her. I shared my confusion and conflict over the two forces that were competing for my attention. I had just broken up with Karen and I was feeling a little despondent and lonely. Bobbi invited me to a meeting that night at a house in Evergreen Park. It was a Christian youth organization of some kind and the topic of conversation was Jesus, Jesus and more Jesus. There were people testifying and there were people who were crying. I didn't get it. The leader of the group asked the new guests to stand up and testify to Jesus. At this point, I was feeling very uncomfortable with all this Jesus business so I ducked out as quickly as I could without being noticed. This was definitely not my cup of tea. I was more of a loner and if I was going to be in a group, it would be a rock band and not a bunch of people saying they were 'born again,' whatever that meant.

While I drove home, west down 95th street through Oak Lawn, it began to rain lightly. The streets were slick, but seemed to glow from the red taillights reflected on the surface. The intermittent wipers were on, the radio was off and, despite all my material success, I was miserable. Suddenly, I heard a voice. Not a human voice that my ears heard, but an inner voice in my head that was distinct from my own thoughts. It must have been the same voice that the apostle Paul heard on the road to Damascus. It was God, and God was telling me what I had been thinking about was true; that I was the reincarnation of Jesus. I began crying and was overcome with emotion. The voice was a confirmation when I needed it most. This was not my imagination and I was not hallucinating because I didn't take drugs. For me, this was real. God was bestowing His/Her blessing upon me and before God went out of my head, God conveyed the words 'master it or it will master you.'

The implication for me was crystal clear. The responsibility of having the soul that was in the physical body of Jesus, now in my body, meant that I had to become fully committed to doing the will of God. The high vibration of this soul was such that, if I did not keep up with its energetic frequency, it would overwhelm me. That is what God meant by the 'master it or it will master you.' I would have to do whatever was required of me. I knew that now. The magnitude of this realization was so monumental, that I came to know and understand that no one on earth would ever believe such a grandiose and narcissistic thing (delusional anyone?) unless I could prove it scientifically and meta-physically, beyond the shadow of a doubt. I had absolute faith that God would lead me in the right direction.

The fact remained, however, that if I did not accept the challenge of verifying this past life as Jesus, the thought of it alone, without scientific validation, would ultimately drive me literally out of my mind. In many ways this is what Jesus experienced when driven to fulfill the prophecies. Think about the similarities.

My subconscious thoughts were now spilling into my present conscious awareness. I now knew, on an intuitive and gut level, who I was in the past. But, how in the world would I be able to verify it? I prayed for God to show me the way and to guide me on this quest. Jesus had been gone physically for two thousand years.

Was there any solid evidence that could link the past life to the present one? I had learned from my study of Qabala that in order to find what I was seeking I needed to empty my cup first, so, I decided to 'let go' and, as they say, 'let God,' i.e. turn it over to God. God would have to show me the way to accomplish this seemingly impossible task. God did. The door opened wide because I knocked hard and I knocked loudly.

I crossed the threshold and entered the inner sanctum of 'heaven on earth.' I was not in some dream world. I was wide awake and consciously aware and headed in a totally new direction. My quest for the '*Holy Grail*' had begun. I would seek the 'meaning of life.' It would become the journey into the nature of my own true self and the adventure was just beginning.

3: The Signs [1974]

By early 1974, I was firmly and solidly on the right path and going in the right direction, but things would again change. One day, I received a call on one of my real estate listings advertised for sale. The buyer's name was Jimmy Lipkowski and I sold him a house. Jimmy owned and operated a successful carry-out pizza parlor and the two of us really hit it off. Jimmy said he was also looking to buy a bar and asked me if I could help him find one. I asked Jimmy if he would be interested in being partners in a rock nightclub and Jimmy said he would. I still had all my connections to the bands from my rock and roll days and, having been in so many clubs over the years, I had a good idea of the type of club I wanted to own and what would be successful. The money in real estate was excellent but, after five years in that business, it had lost some of its challenge and I was itching to get back into entertainment in some way. The lifestyle, with its late nights, girls, music and glamor, was still in my blood.

Despite the 'God' experience in 1973, and my commitment to the spiritual way, I was still very much 'of this world.' I was still studying metaphysics and I was without a serious relationship, which I really wanted, so I thought by opening up a nightclub I could maximize my chances of meeting my soul mate. I was right.

Although I was committed to my spiritual quest, I was no monk or priest and would never be. I loved women far too much and loved being in their company. After reading *'Be Here Now'* by Baba Ram Das in 1972, I 'got it;' i.e. 'being here now,' living only in the present moment in time. It was like 1969 when I learned Tao meant how. I was going to live life to the fullest and pursue every dream. My focus was sharper. My senses were crisper. My intellect had become keener. My intuition was stronger and I was able to perceive situations clearly. In short, I was becoming more God-conscious. But, unbeknownst to me, my journey to recognition of my discovery of the past life would be many, many miles long, and many years into the future. Had I known how many years into the future, I may have been too discouraged to continue the quest.

You could say my past life journey officially began when God spoke to me in 1973, but my material existence was quite a spectacle. I traded in my 1972 Mark IV for a new 1973 mustard color Mark IV with a brown sun roof and 'pimped' it out with amber fog lamps and my name, stenciled onto the doors in twenty-two karat gold leaf. Inside the car, under the glove box, I installed a psychedelic light show. I was materially polluted and the perfect candidate for change.

Yes, we can change, and we all must change our perspective from gross materialism to spirituality.

I began my search for a location for the nightclub. My vision was clear. I wanted a 1930's era elegant bistro with a hard rock format and a disco. I knew it would be successful, so I looked for a location that offered an abundance of parking and a cabaret liquor license, i.e. a 4:00 a.m. license. Cruising south on Cicero Ave, in Burbank, Illinois, I spotted a big lounge in a shopping center, right next door to a big supermarket. There was parking for hundreds of cars and, at night, the entire center was closed down. It was the perfect location. Right across the street was Goldblatt's Department Store, so it had great exposure.

The place was called the *Willow Tree Lounge*. It had 4,000 square feet of interior space and a cabaret license, and it was for sale. The place had almost no business. It was tired and very rundown. The only redeeming things were the huge bar that extended diagonally out into the lounge, and the huge willow tree behind the bar. There was a real tree trunk, bark and all, that went floor to ceiling and the ceiling was fairly high. There were imitation willow branches that extended out on the ceiling in all directions, enshrouding the entire club in a verdant canopy of green. It was beautiful and gave the place an indoor/outdoor feeling. Sitting at the bar was like being in the forest. It was spectacular.

For $30,000, we bought a bar, a tree and a lease. Everything else became trash. Jimmy's brother Rick was a carpenter and Mike, who became the manager, and their friends gutted the place. The liquor was included in the sale, but most were cheap brands we would never serve. There was one case of liquor that had never been opened, which turned out to be a treasure for years to come; an orange liquor like *Grand Marnier,* but smoother. The liquor was called *Mandarin Napoleon* and it tasted wonderful. Oh the joys of the material world.

Now that the location had been secured, I put my vision to work. I went antique shopping. I named the club after Jean Harlow, the blond eccentric bombshell from the 1930's. *Harlow's Bistro and Discotheque* soon became the talk of the town. At each corner of the bar (there were four corners), hung a beautiful imitation *Tiffany* lamp. I met Fred Sperry who was a freelance artist who happened to work for the company *Foster and Kleiser* who owned most of the billboards in Chicago. Fred had painted the Dewer's Scotch ad with the glass and ice cubes. He painted those billboards and made them look like photographs. Armed with a full color illustrated book on the movie stars of the 1930's, I hired Fred to replicate many of them in huge paintings that I hung throughout the club. Fred painted portraits of Jean Harlow, Norma Talmadge, Bessie Love, Mae West and other movie stars of that legendary Hollywood Era.

A big stage was built and behind it were huge plate glass windows, adorned with red swag draperies. Next to the stage was a very large wall where Fred painted a profile of Jean Harlow's face with a large border. Around the border were 'chase lights,' the kind found on outdoor electronic marquees. Above the dance floor, directly in front of the stage, was a big, mirrored disco ball, illuminated by two beams of light. Against the wall was a reproduction Wurlitzer 1930's jukebox with the rainbow that lit up.

The wall-to-wall carpeting was a commercial grade in red and black, with a pattern popular in the 1930's. There were antiques everywhere: an old 'pot-belly' stove that nestled in one of the hidden corners, antique tables and floor lamps. In my antique shopping, I found a stained glass window from a one-hundred-year-old church in Wisconsin. It was at least ten feet high and was a depiction of the Mother Mary cradling a lamb in her arms: 'The lamb of Christ.' What are the chances?

I also had the good fortune to buy seven of the leaded glass windows from Al Capone's house in Barrington, Illinois. (That was the story I was told). The tall stained glass window and the 'Capone' windows went in the foyer of the club. I had the windows covered in thick plexiglass to prevent breakage in the event of fights, which happened often on occasion.

A big solid brass cash register in the foyer entry sat on an antique pedestal and there was a big wing-backed chair that I recovered in red velvet. I would sit in that chair, many an evening, checking out the girls who came through those magic portals.

All the men, including Jimmy and myself wore 1930's-style black tuxedos, custom made by *Seno* formal wear. The tuxedo shirts were wing tip and we wore black bow ties. The waitresses wore long gowns. There were tables next to the dance floor and there were two elevated seating sections that were even in height with the stage. There was a very large section on one side of the bar and a smaller section on the other; red tablecloths and votive candles on each table. There were Harlow napkins and Harlow buttons, which were given out by the thousands.

The bar featured Heineken and Augsburger beer on draft. There was a black bar menu with gold tassel, that featured forty-eight imported bottled bears from around the world and a fairly decent wine list, which was affordable. The bar glasses were a 1930's art deco stem ware that hung upside down around the entire bar. All drinks were served in stemware; very elegant but very impractical. Art for art's sake.

Most well drinks were $1.50 and the imported beers were $2.00. I believed in fair prices and knew people would appreciate that. The southwest side was home to working class people who could not afford north side prices. Better to sell three drinks for $4.50 than one for three bucks. People returned in droves. The regulars were a loyal bunch.

The cover charge on the weekend was only $2.00 and a dress code was strictly enforced. There were 'bikers' in the area who were often looking for trouble, so the dress code acted as a deterrent to their admission. The customers liked the idea of dressing up. Harlow's immediately attracted the 'beautiful people,' who came from all parts of the city. Beautiful people, great rock and roll and reasonable prices: a winning combination; Harlow's immediately became a huge success.

The rock band's first set began at 10:00 p.m. and the last set ended at 3:15 a.m. I would always announce the bands and warm up the crowd, describing coming entertainment, special concert nights or Jam nights. Harlow's was a real nightclub and I was comfortable on stage. Sometimes, I would jam with the band, but not too often. During the band breaks, I would spin records from the disco booth in the back of the club on the upper tier and I would always be studying spiritual things. For me, this was the roaring 70's.

The band *Chicago,* once called *CTA (Chicago Transit Authority)*, opened up their own night club, called *B'Ginnings*, in Schaumberg, Illinois, a far northwest suburb of the city. *B'Ginnings* had a 1:00 a.m. license and people would make the drive to Harlow's to keep the party going. Sometimes, some of the band from *Chicago* would come in and jam. Harlow's had quite a reputation for the best bands in Chicago.

About a month before Harlow's opened, on April 1, 1974, I flooded the entire southwest side of Chicago and suburbs with 10,000 paper flyers. Word spread like wild fire that a real hard rock nightclub was opening. The only other places for great rock music in Chicago were Rush Street, the near north side, or the far north and northwest suburbs.

On opening night, the eve of my twenty-sixth birthday, Pezband played, starring Clifford Johnson, (without doubt one of the best dance bands in Chicago). They were a favorite on Rush Street and they always brought the house down. Doors opened at 8:00 p.m. and, if you wanted to get in on a Friday or Saturday night, you needed to get there early. On opening night, a long line formed early and remained for hours.

A two-hour wait to get in was not unusual because, once in, very few people left. Why leave? Harlow's was almost always jam-packed on the weekends. Last call for alcohol was at 3:15 A.M., when the band finished its last set. Lights went up at 3:45 A.M., and the club needed to be empty promptly at 4:00 A.M. The money was dropped into the floor safe in the cloakroom and everybody went for sunrise breakfast at *Lorelei's* in Oak Lawn. This was the most fun I had ever had in my life.

4: First Miracles?

After a few months of success at Harlow's, I began to change my mode of attire. The more I studied mysticism, the more I changed. I delved much deeper into astrology and it seemed as if the books which held certain answers were being literally thrown at me from all directions. (Astrology is the study that assumes and attempts to interpret the influence of the sun, moon and planets on human affairs, and human personality. Without our solar system human beings would not exist. It is the combined energy of the heavenly bodies that literally make up a human being's personality, character and individuality which are preserved lifetime to lifetime. Astrology is the record of the personality of those lifetimes.)

As soon as I finished one book and had my questions answered, the next book would appear with more answers. It never ceased to amaze me how this happened. Having been an English major in college made my research easier. I had the skills and, after God intervened in my life in 1973, I metamorphosed from a researcher into an investigative reporter. I had a lead on a great story and I was going to get to the bottom of it. I was determined to 'master it' and not let 'it' master me.

Being the reincarnation of Jesus is not to be confused with having the Christ energy, inherent in every human being. Many saints and mystics experienced this 'Christ' energy and were able to perform miraculous healings; some could levitate and one mystical Saint allegedly could fly. With this strong vibration, 'all things are possible.' Jesus employed this 'Christ' energy and that is why he is improperly called Jesus 'Christ' instead of Jesus 'the' Christ. Any human being can achieve this Christ vibration simply by becoming the embodiment of Love, which is what God is all about.

Some people who have tapped into this Christ energy frequency think they are Jesus. This is not my situation, based on the documented evidence. I actually lived the life of the real person called Jesus (of Nazareth) and at the preordained and pre-appointed time, Jesus reincarnated into the new (flesh) body of Bruce, who was descended from the bloodline of Jesus through his first-born daughter, Tamar Damaris. Dan Brown, in his book *The Da Vinci Code*, erroneously claims Jesus' first-born daughter was named

Sarah. The biblical record and the *Dead Sea Scrolls* do not support this claim.

In the late 1960's, I worked at *India Gifts and Foods* on Belmont Avenue in Chicago. I felt a strong connection to people from India. I bought my first sitar (a musical instrument made popular by Ravi Shankar), Indian shirts and lots of incense. I stopped wearing the tuxedo at Harlow's and began wearing Indian shirts and a red beanie cap (like the guru, Bhagwan Shree Rajneesh). I grew my beard back, my hair got even longer and I was receiving ever more frequent poetic transmissions.

I didn't sleep much anymore. I would go to sleep at 6:30 or 7:00 A.M. and be up four to five hours later, filled with energy. One weekend night, away from the city lights, I looked up at the starry night sky and asked God for a 'sign.' Jews are always looking for a 'sign.' "God," I said, "Give me a sign that my being the reincarnation of Jesus is true." Obviously, it wasn't enough that God had spoken to me the year before. I still had huge doubts and rightfully so. If you told someone that God spoke to you, you would be branded delusional. If you told them God confirmed that you were Jesus in a past life, well, you were crazy. Now, at the very instant I asked God for a sign, a shooting star streaked across the sky. Coincidence? Timing is everything.

That shooting star brought back a memory from when I was age ten. I had suffered from a very serious hernia that was bulging out of my groin. My cousin, Nathan Zimmerman, chief surgeon at *Columbus Hospital* (on the north side), had examined me a few days before. Dr. Zimmerman had told my mom to get me to the hospital as soon as possible so I could be operated on before the hernia ruptured. It was very swollen and protruded ominously. When my mom checked me in at the hospital, Nathan examined me again. My urgent operation had to wait until morning, because I needed a good night's sleep in order to be rested. Nathan obviously believed I would live through the night.

I was Nathan's first surgery for the day. The nurse came in to check on me one more time and was shocked to find that the hernia, which had been close to rupture, had completely disappeared. It was my first healing and I performed it on myself. There is no medical explanation why a disease suddenly goes into remission; it just disappears. Did being ten years old have something to do with it?

A few weeks after the opening of Harlow's, I was driving south on Harlem Ave. Sitting outside on an automobile dealership lot was a sports car I had never seen before in my life. I did a double take, made a U-turn, went into the showroom and asked about the car. It was a 1971 *Maserati Ghibli Spyder.* Italian, gorgeous, sexy, irresistible; burgundy, tan leather interior, chrome spoked wheels, dual gas tanks, four overhead camshafts, four dual Weber carburetors: a nightmare on wheels.

One of the most beautiful automobiles in the world was sitting outside in the elements and rotting away. With only 21,000 miles on the odometer this car was tired. Whoever owned it before had lots of fun with it, and car enthusiast that I was, I had to own it. I made the best deal I could and bought it on the spot: I could be very impulsive. That car became the object of a love/hate relationship that would last fourteen years.

Even Jaguar XKE's could not compare to this car in the hassle factor. No one in Chicago seemed to know how to work on it. The Ferrari dealership on the near north side declined to work on a Maserati. Other independent foreign car specialists however "saw me coming". When asked if they could tune the four dual carbs. They said, 'Yes we can!' Can you calibrate the four overhead cams? 'Yes we can!' It was always 'Yes we can' and my money slowly dribbled away.

This car required a study in patience, persistence, and determination and I would learn the vicissitudes of owning a class of automobile that was really out of my league. However, my automobile of destiny was part of the material process of manifesting 'signs,' which made me more confident that I was going in the right direction. How could a Maserati sports car possibly be an indication that I was on the right path? Why wasn't I in an ashram or a monastery or studying to be a rabbi, for that matter? Now, that would be the spiritual thing to do, wouldn't it?

I didn't notice right away but on the reverse suede dashboard, on the driver's side, below the windshield, was a small thin shiny metal strip that had the car's serial number stamped on it. Next to the last number was the symbol of the Jewish Star of David with a circle around it. Years later, I saw the very same symbol in a book by James Churchward published in the 1930's: The symbol was an ancient Babylonian cosmogram. Just two years before on Maui the shirt with the Star of David had found me and now, a car! Amazing coincidence? The Maserati has as its symbol the Trident of Neptune. In astrology Neptune represents the mystical forces at work in our solar system. The car, like the shirt, was 'meant to be.' There are no accidents in life; no coincidences, only synchronistic events that defy scientific explanation.

I soon learned that it wasn't the ownership of material things that mattered; it was the attachment to those things. I received another poetic transmission, called *Matter*. The lesson for me was in detachment. The more I detached, the freer I became, and the freer I became, the more my vibration increased. The higher my vibration became, the more fine-tuned my frequency, which created a magnetic pull. This magnetism drew everything I needed to myself, whether it was a car, a shirt, a book, a woman or anything. It's the way the universe works and it is the same for everyone, with no exception. Increase your energetic vibration and increase your magnetism: The Law of Attraction. If you raise your vibration, things will come. How do you raise it? Love more. [Christ-mas. Christ = Love and Mas = more]. Just love more and it will come. That is the secret of becoming who you truly are. We can all re-create ourselves by loving more.

One morning, after Harlow's closed and getting light out, my assistant manager, Bob, was having some extreme emotional problems. We were standing in the parking lot in front of the club. I was reading a new book by Richard Bach called *Jonathan Livingston Seagull,* a book about self-transcendence and transformation and I was telling Bob the story of Jonathan: how we all must transcend our earthly limitations and attachments that we have placed upon ourselves and transform our present reality to one in tune with the pulse of the universe.

We talked for nearly an hour, standing in the parking lot and it was light by now. The exact moment I finished telling Bob about Jonathan, a huge, white seagull swooped down, not more than a hundred feet from where we were standing. While Bob's jaw literally dropped, I was 'stirred but not shaken.'

Another 'coincidence,' you might say. I was reading a book about a seagull and a seagull landed right in front of me. However, as Lake Michigan was at least twenty-five miles to the east, what was a pure white seagull doing in Burbank, Illinois, at that exact moment in time? Of all the thousands of places to land, why there? Why then? The universe was demonstrating to me how it works. Synchronistic events are difficult to explain in a non-spiritual manner. Just write it off as coincidence, right?

The Fourth of July was quickly approaching and my parents were spending the long weekend at *George Williams College* in Lake Geneva, Wisconsin. They invited my brother Craig and me to come and visit. It would be a welcome break from the frenzy of *Harlow's* and the city. I picked up my brother in the Maserati and made the two plus hour trip without incident.

The wooded campus was luscious. The towering oaks and whispering pines foretold a weekend of solace and serenity. The shimmering lake was inviting and the whole place had a spiritual presence. It was wonderful seeing my whole family together, which didn't happen often, anymore. Everyone staying at the college settled in for a good old BBQ and fireworks on the lake after the sun went down and the last rays of daylight paled into darkness. It was fun to watch, with the ooohs and the aahs and the wows of the display.

By 10:00 p.m. most everyone else had gone to sleep. But, as I was a night owl now, going to sleep at this hour was unthinkable. The sounds of the insects, the croaking of the frogs and the 'who who' of an occasional owl were all that could be heard. In the moonless night I walked out to the end of the pier. I laid down on my back and gazed at the billions of stars and the Milky Way appeared like white cotton candy, spread across the sky. The constellations were easily identifiable. The heavens were magnificent: God's creation. It was just me and God out there at the end of the pier and, even though I thought it inappropriate, I would ask God one last time for confirmation. The Chinese Book of Oracle *(I Ching)* calls this asking without good cause, 'Youthful Folly.' I already knew the answer; asking again just might test God's patience, but ask I did.

"God, am I really the reincarnation of Jesus? This is very intense and I am in very deep here and I just want to make sure that what you told me was true." Instantly the night sky lit up from one end of the lake to the other in a huge arch of brilliant heavenly lights. This was truly an act of God. The shirts, the shooting star, the sea gull, the Maserati and now, this. What could be grander than this? What are the chances of this occurrence at that exact moment in time? Asking God a direct question and getting such a response!

From that moment, I changed yet again. I was now a true believer in myself, my mission on earth and my destiny. God told me to 'master it' and "by God," that is what I intended to do.

Are signs miracles? Or are miracles signs?

"Healings are not to be viewed as miraculous occurrences because all spiritual healing, at its core, is self-healing. It is a manifestation of prayer, concentrated and focused thought, directed intensely at the self and the universe, which demands to be whole. "Go, be it done to you as you have believed."

The healing I had brought upon myself at age ten was exactly this. I wanted, with all my heart, to be made whole and I was healed. I believed, in my ten-year-old mind, and it was done.

5: Numbers of Destiny

By August 1974, Harlow's established itself as Chicago's premier rock club. Everything was running smoothly: Jimmy ran the back of the house, i.e. the money, the books, the ordering and the bar. When the bouncers violated the fire code and the place was packed to the gills, Jimmy and I were behind the bar trying to keep up with the demand for drinks. I learned every facet of running a nightclub, except bouncing.

As the material side of my life prospered, my spiritual side flourished as well. I came into possession of the book, *The Aquarian Gospel of Jesus the Christ of the Piscean Age* by Levi, published in 1895, which explained what an 'age' was, what the Piscean and Aquarian Ages were, what the word Christ meant, the relationship between Jesus and the Christ and what the Akashic records were. The word Aquarius (the age we are in now) is derived from the Latin word aqua, meaning water, with Aquarius being the Water Bearer. The symbol of the sign? A man carrying a pitcher of water in his right hand. In this book, Jesus referred to the beginning of the Aquarian age with the words: "And then the man who bears the pitcher of water will walk forth across an arc of heaven; the sign and signet of the Son of Man will stand forth in the eastern sky. The wise will then lift up their heads and know that the redemption of the earth is near." *157:29-30.*

I recognized that as the reincarnation of Jesus I was the representation of the *Son of Man* of the Aquarian age and explained as much, in a letter to Shirley MacLaine (without disclosing that I was the reincarnation of Jesus).

Within one month of the Aurora Borealis confirmation at Lake Geneva, I came to *The Aquarian Gospel* and the wealth of information it contained: the Akashic records of the lost eighteen years of Jesus' life and a clue that would open up another dimension of understanding, preparing me for what would come in December, 1976. Jesus said: "You know that all my life was one great **drama** for the sons of men; a **pattern** for the sons of men. I lived to show the possibilities of man. What I have done all men can do, and what I am all men shall be." *178:43-46.*

The Akashic records are not in any library on earth. It took the author, Levi, forty years of meditation and study to enter the superfine ethers of spiritual consciousness where the records are stored. It is a vibrational place and not an actual physical location. The records are in a different dimensional reality, vibrating at a rate so high that the only way to access them is by vibrating at the same frequency, like tuning into a particular radio station with a clear signal and no static.

The word Christ, for example, means the anointed one and is an official title that carries a particular vibration. Anyone can achieve this vibration if willing to work for it; i.e. follow the cosmic rules to achieve it. The Akashic Records contain every thought of every soul that has ever lived. During Jesus' life, every thought and deed were recorded in those records. His personality, like all human personalities, was reduced to planetary frequencies of energy. These energies are recorded and become our astrological horoscope, which is our **pattern**, script and drama: merely a record of our past lives. The *Aquarian Gospel of Jesus the Christ* catapulted me into a new realm of spiritual understanding.

One night at the club, a close associate of the band Chicago extended an invitation to me to stay at Chicago's Ranch, in Nederland, Colorado. I jumped at the chance, invited a friend and we drove the Maserati out to Colorado. The ranch was called *The Caribou*. Upon arrival I asked where the band was and was directed to their studio. Several of the band members were there including Lee, one of the horn players. We were asked: "Who are you and why are you here? Somewhat taken aback, I said: "The band's business manager, John Brakamanus, invited me out here for a visit." Someone said, "no one told us about this and you must leave now."

My first Rocky Mountain high ended when I got stopped for speeding, doing ninety in sixty-five miles per hour zone. Something wasn't right. My life had been smooth as silk; this was the first glitch. Colorado was my first long trip in the car. On the way home during a blinding rainstorm the windshield wipers broke so I tailgated a 16 wheeler preventing the rain from obstructing my vision. Through the white knuckles and tense moments, I remained resolute in knowing that God was watching over me.

After the Fourth of July Aurora Borealis experience, I felt invincible and not in an arrogant way. Rather, I sensed that I had a shield of divine protection. After all, I believed, I had been Jesus and that must count for something. This line of reasoning would get me in great deal of trouble in the future and I mean a great deal of trouble.

The rock and roll bands, *Brother Bait, Beowulf, The Pezband, Joe Jammer, Cheap Trick,* and *H.P. Lovecraft* performed at Harlow's. We booked the top groups from the mid-west and as far away as Atlanta, Georgia and these bands had a following. This was the most non-stop excitement I ever experienced. Playing in a band was nothing compared to this. Every night was change and something different. There were always beautiful young women and I was still fairly young myself. God had His plans and an agenda for me to keep. It was up to me to reveal a facet of God's Intelligent Design for humanity. Many are called to do this. Each in his or her own way. I was being guided in my way.

The Aquarian Gospel of Jesus the Christ activated past life memories in me. There was even a passage nearly identical to one of my poems in *Messiah For Hire* that I wrote before I read the book.

Up to the years when Jesus taught the elders in the temple, around the age of twelve, until his baptism by John at the age of thirty, Jesus traveled to most of the countries in the Middle and Far East and studied with spiritual masters (gurus). These are called the "Lost Eighteen Years" that do not appear in the *New Testament*. Alexandria, Egypt at the time was a great center for learning and the library there was said to contain all the mysteries and wisdom of the cosmos. Jesus spent much time there studying according to the "Gospel."

He also studied in China, Tibet and India, under the guidance of the greatest living masters. He learned how to 'astral travel' (out of body), meditate, heal and to tap into the universal consciousness of the Creator. All the things he learned in life plus those eighteen years he would carry into his next life.

From the Torah Scholars, he learned we are all created in the image and likeness of God, but that we have forgotten this. From the Essenes at Qumran by the Dead Sea, Jesus learned higher levels of astrology, numerology and Qabala. He learned the mysteries encoded in the Torah that foretold all future events as potentialities. 2000 years later physicists using high-speed computer technology discovered this Bible Code.

In Greece, Jesus studied Plato, Socrates, Aristotle and Pythagoras and learned sacred geometry and numerology. He learned from the Egyptians their mysteries and secrets about the afterlife and how the soul judges itself after death (earth-life) based on its past life(s) actions. He learned about the Sumerians, the oldest known civilization, who were taught by the alien Annunaki about cloning and genetic engineering some three hundred thousand years before, and how they created Homo sapiens using "stock" from Homo erectus that proliferated at that time. The "let **us** create man in **our** own image" in *Genesis 1:26-27* clears up the mystery.

The Aquarian Gospel quickened my spirit even more. I was vibrating faster now. I stopped drinking alcohol for several months, (no easy task while owning a nightclub), began long fasts (some two weeks), practiced Hatha yoga, ate vegetarian (but only briefly), lost twenty-five pounds and began jogging every day. I was on a mission and going to fulfill my destiny.

In October, my brother Craig was planning a hiking trip to the White Mountains of New Hampshire and suggested I go along. Craig calculated that with the summer and fall rush of hikers gone, we would have the mountains to ourselves. He was right. No one was crazy enough to go into the mountains in late October. When we had climbed to a fairly high altitude, the wind whipped up and it began snowing. The temperatures dropped to sub-zero after the sun set. I pounded my feet and hands all night long to keep the blood circulating; I did not want to die in my sleep. Somehow we made it through the night and Craig decided to take me back down the mountain to *Franconia College* and to civilization. Winter hiking was not for me. Craig thrived on this type of dangerous adventure and returned to the mountains by himself. He said he would see me in a few days and to just hang tight at the college. The hand of God was at work.

There was a numerologist at the school, teaching a small class which I attended. I learned more about my destiny and mission through my numbers. My destiny number was calculated by adding the month, day and year of my birth. I was born on April 2, 1948 (four (4th month) plus two plus one plus nine plus four plus eight, adds up to the number twenty-eight [28]). The sum total of those numbers is ten. I learned that our names have numerical vibrations.

The teacher taught the Pythagorean system of numerology, which seemed familiar to me. I learned that my name consisted of two master numbers, twenty-two (22) and thirty-three (33) and the number eight, (8) which is the number of (spiritual) power. The cipher is in Decoding the *Prologue.*

Jesus corresponded to the master number eleven (11), albeit a double eleven (explained later). I had evolved from a number eleven as Jesus, to number twenty-two and number thirty-three as Bruce. My numbers past and present were now in perfect order of cosmic chronology and reflected my evolution numerologically. My destiny numbers, the two and the eight, (28), the sum total of 4-2-1948, means cooperation with one's own self with power to create a new beginning. This made perfect sense to me and strengthened my past life beliefs even more. The numerology teacher said the numbers always match the person's astrology chart. I would soon find this to be true.

Upon my return to Chicago, I consulted a professional astrologer to have my horoscope chart done. Laurie Brady was a locally famous celebrity astrologer. She asked me in advance of our session for all my birth information; i.e., April 2, 1948 at 8:38 A.M. in Chicago, Illinois.

Laurie lived at *Lake Point Tower* in Chicago's downtown off Lake Shore Drive. She was a flaming redhead, quite attractive who dressed rather provocatively.

Her apartment was ornate, with commanding views of the city and Lake Michigan.

When the session began she turned on her tape recorder. Much of what she said didn't make sense to me. It didn't sound like me at all. She did say, however, that I was probably a disciple of Jesus. I accepted what she had to say but I was troubled by it.

Disciple? That couldn't be right. That was contrary to what God told me and contrary to the 'signs' I had been given. For six months, I pondered this astrological chart. Something wasn't right. The teacher at *Franconia College* said the numbers match the astrology but my numbers didn't match the chart and I was confused. It just didn't add up. I discovered six months later after having a computerized horoscope done for my birth date that Laurie Brady made a huge error when she did my chart. She converted the time of my birth from 8:38 A.M. to 8:38 P.M. That changed everything. None of the energies were right. In retrospect that error was meant to be as the computerized horoscope opened so many more spiritual doors. There are no accidents in the universe. There are reasons for everything and all for our soul's growth.

In November 1974, another important book came into my life; *The Secret Doctrines of Jesus,* by H. Spencer Lewis, first published in 1937. This book confirmed what I had read in the *Aquarian Gospel of Jesus the Christ,* i.e. that Jesus was the Christ, as in *"a"* Christ, and not Jesus 'Christ,' which separates him from being human as we all are. The Church of Rome created "Jesus Christ," the supernatural God-man, the *Son of God,* and not **a** son of God as we all are. We are all God's children.

I learned from *The Secret Doctrines of Jesus* that women were Jesus' disciples, which meant that the Church deliberately evaded this fact. There was an inner circle of an inner circle to which he taught the greatest secrets and mysteries...like reincarnation! The church has fought hard, over the centuries, to keep these truths from the masses. The seals of *Revelation* have been loosened and the information is no longer a mystery or secret.

Jesus secretly taught the divine principles (the ones being taught in this book.) The fact remains: If the Christian church of today, which includes the *Church of Rome,* made itself aware of the secret knowledge and then took the time to teach it to the world, the church could become a powerful influence in the world today for peace, joy, happiness, health and spiritual contentment. Unfortunately, it hasn't and it won't. It will not renounce its archaic condemnation of reincarnation. It will not teach the meaning of astrology and the esoteric meta-sciences that these secrets and mysteries that Jesus taught entail. The "church" has not grown; it has regressed. It teaches the masses very little and the masses as a result are still living in spiritual darkness. They know very little spiritually.

Jesus announced, very early in his mission, that he did not agree with or support many of the ideas of the Jewish faith. Thus, he attracted antagonism and animus to himself and as a result most of the Jews assumed he could not be the long awaited Messiah. They wanted an establishment messiah; not a spiritual revolutionary that called them out on their hypocrisy.

The Law of Karma was another one of Jesus' secret doctrines, based on the law of cause and effect, which he taught as 'what you sow you reap.'

6: The Law of Attraction Really Works

The Christmas season came, Harlow's was decorated and everyone else was of good cheer, except me. I was feeling lonely and incomplete, without a girlfriend. The messages in my poetry were streaming through, trying to tell me something, but what? I didn't feel alone; I simply missed being *in love*. Loving someone made me feel complete, whole, fulfilled and able to demonstrate what I felt in my heart.

I met many women after Carol and I divorced. I loved being in love. Loving God was not enough. I believed that being in a meaningful relationship helped make me complete. A Jewish Rabbi, for example, is required to be married because marriage is one of the greatest teachers; from it, we can learn how to love, to share, to give and to be intimate. It allows us to express the Divine. For me, this was true.

I had heard about the spiritual concept of soul mates, i.e. someone we have lived with, been associated with or been in love with before, in other lifetimes. I learned family members and dear friends can be soul mates, both male and female. Since we have lived many lifetimes, we have been involved with many different souls. Some souls even make a pact never to separate because of an intense love between them and, most likely, those souls find each other in a subsequent lifetime.

Depending upon the lessons to be learned, a past life lover can become one's mother, sister, brother or father. A daughter can become a daughter again or a brother, mother, or even a lover. There are many lessons to be learned between soul mates and the combinations are varied and vast. The messages I was receiving seemed to point to meeting a soul mate, but that was not happening. I could manifest shirts, shooting stars, cars, seagulls, and even the *Northern Lights*. However, amongst all the beautiful women streaming through Harlow's, I didn't recognize any as having spent time with me in the past. I could only maintain my faith and believe that God would provide.

Intuitively, I knew I was getting closer to meeting that certain someone. I was studying hard, fasting, praying and doing everything I could to raise my vibration, in preparation for our reunion. She was coming, and coming soon.

Saturday night, January 31, 1975. I was off work for the weekend. Inspired by the reincarnation poems that were coming through, I wrote a song, *'Reflections of Like Mind And Soul,'* about a lover (possibly a wife) from a past life. None of the women I was dating fit the description. The song described a particular person I was going to meet, but when?

Early Sunday evening, intuition told me to go to the club, something I rarely did on my nights off. Five nights of intensity and deafening music were enough but the voice within told me to go. So, I asked out a girl I liked, called the club and told Jimmy I was coming in. Jimmy said, "Why? It's your night off, take a break." When I insisted, Jimmy promised to reserve a table and mentioned that our booking agent was stopping by and making the rounds to all the clubs he booked. Harlow's was his top club.

Shortly after the band started their first set, the booking agent arrived. On his arm was the most beautiful woman I had ever seen and I instantly recognized her as the one I had written the song for the night before. It was her: I knew it to the core of my being.

They approached our table and introductions were made; *she* sat down next to me. Despite the loud music, I looked directly into her eyes and smiled. She smiled back. Michael (the agent) told her that the owner of the club was sitting right next to her, between the two women. *Elise* was her name. The music was too loud to talk; everyone listened and watched the band. I was dying to talk to her but there was nothing I could do or say. I had a date and I assumed she was the agent's girlfriend.

At the end of the band's set, Michael rose to leave, as he had other bands to check on that night at other clubs. It was quieter now and as Elise was about to get up, I leaned over and whispered in her ear, "Michael is really lucky to have you." That was it; they'd been there for a half hour and then they were gone. I was heartsick: I could not get Elise out of my mind. She was all I thought about.

After my date went home, I told Jimmy what happened. "What am I going to do? I don't have her number. She's going out with Michael. I can't call him for her number, he wouldn't give it to me." All I could do was focus my mind on Elise. I thought of nothing else but seeing Elise in my presence. I knew what visualization was and I knew I had the power to manifest whatever I needed in my quest to re-create who I was. I knew I was the creator of my life and that I was the master of my own fate. I stayed on at the club alone for one more set and relived the first time my eyes had met hers, still totally convinced that she was the object of the song.

I had a red eye flight the following night to Tucson, Arizona where my parents were spending the winter and taking classes at the university. They invited me to visit for a few days. The timing was perfect. Maybe the trip would help me to get my mind off Elise. Maybe I could get some rest, because she was all I thought about. Love will do that to a person. Create unrest.

It was February 2nd. The night flight to Tucson left from Chicago's *Midway Airport* on the mid-southwest side. The plane was nearly empty. It was bitter cold outside, but there was no snow. The runways were clear and no deicing was necessary. Why, then, was the plane not taxiing down the runway and getting ready to take off? It was just sitting there. There were no announcements from the Captain saying there was going to be a delay due to some hitherto unknown mechanical problem. Nothing! I was still thinking about Elise. If we were airborne I could at least settle in to reading and forget about her for a while.

I was getting a little antsy, looking down the aisle toward the front of the cabin to see if there was anything unusual going on. Somebody walked on and then moved quickly down the aisle. It was a woman with dark hair, long coat, and carrying a tennis racket. As she came closer, I thought she looked familiar. It was Elise, the object of my constant thoughts.

My eyes met hers: "Oh my God!" I can hardly believe this". This was my best manifestation yet. I created this reality. (Co-created). My thoughts got Elise on that plane. After an intense eye-to-eye exchange she said, "I need to get to my seat" and proceeded down the aisle. Moments later, a man rushed by and headed toward where Elise was seated.

My head was spinning with excitement. I didn't know what it was called at the time, but I had drawn Elise to me through the power of my thoughts. I had done it with the seagull, the Maserati, the t-shirts and the Northern Lights. The magnetic shooting star power of my will attracted these things into material manifestation. There is no other way to explain it. Coincidence must be ruled out.

Half an hour later, I had not read one word of my book. Someone tapped me on my shoulder. "Would you like to join us in the back?" Elise said. "Sure." I went back to visit with Elise and she introduced me to Ross, a friend with whom she had met the previous summer. She hadn't seen or talked to this guy until he unexpectedly called her the morning after we met to invite her to Tucson for a long weekend.

Elise confided in me that she really didn't like Michael (the booking agent) and wasn't his girlfriend. As to their tardy arrival, she explained that she and Ross lived far north on the opposite side of the city. He mis-calculated the time needed to get there. Even more unexpectedly, there were no flights to Tucson leaving out of Chicago's *O' Hare Airport* (which wasn't far from where they each lived). Ross somehow managed to have the airline hold the plane! How often does an airline do that? God was at work; destiny was at work. Fate had intervened and brought us together… again!

Elise, in the center seat, explained to Ross how we had just met the night before at my nightclub and now, just a little over twenty-four hours later, we are on the same night flight to Tucson. This was truly amazing: beyond belief, even. To anybody else it would have been just a big coincidence, which is what it was to Ross. Coincidence? I knew better. In 1975, mystics would have labeled this event the manifestation of 'mind control' or 'mind over matter.' Now, it's called the *Law of Attraction*. Whatever you call it, it works!

When Elise and I finally had our very first conversation sitting on that plane between Ross and I myself, I learned she was Jewish like me. As we talked we discovered we were born at the same *Lying In* Hospital on the University of Chicago campus. Ross was scratching his head and wondering what the heck was going on. "Who is this, guy? And why is this happening?"

We then discovered we each loved animals: I had a dog and Elise had a dog; I had four cats and Elise had two; my dog was named *Tasha* and her cat was named *Tasha*. She went to *Roosevelt High School*. (I learned, years later, that my cousin, Iris Zimmerman's locker was right next to Elise's). I went to *Roosevelt University*. What are the odds? What is the statistical probability of these occurrences? Just coincidence?

When it was time for me to go back to my seat, I said goodnight and wished them a great weekend. Once again, I failed to get her number. The plane landed and the three of us deplaned together. At the bottom of the escalator, my parents were waiting. After hugs and kisses, I introduced them to Ross and Elise. My mother exclaimed, "You know, I never told you this Bruce, but if you had been born a girl, Louis and I were going to name you Elise." Elise and I looked at each other in absolute, utter amazement. Things were moving very fast.

That night I was so excited I couldn't sleep. I took my pen and writing pad and went to get a bite to eat at *Bob's Big boy Restaurant* because when I was inspired like this, the poems came gushing through. The first poem came through at 1:20 A.M. Then another and then another. I called these A *Trilogy for Elise*. Beethoven must have been so inspired when he wrote his famous *Fur Elise*.

The next day, visiting Elise and Ross out by the pool (she called and invited me) I wrote poems for her on cocktail napkins. It was a great day, being so close to her; so near, yet so far away.

They invited me to drive down with them to *Sonora, Mexico*, the closest border town to Tucson. We ate lunch at a local Mexican restaurant and explored the shops. I could speak some Spanish, which helped in the negotiating process. Later, Ross went to get the car, leaving us alone together for the first time. We embraced and kissed right there in a tourist shop. The sales person asked if we were getting married. Only newlyweds kissed like that in public. I could hardly believe this was happening but I understood why. Ross came with the car and we left for Tucson. Elise was in the passenger seat up front and I was seated directly behind her. It was a full moon. Elise reached back with her right hand and we held hands all the way back to my motel. It was magic, just pure magic. "Do you believe in magic?"

I finally got Elise's phone number, and promised to call her when she returned from Tucson to Chicago. I even spent some quality time with my parents and they were happy that I was happy. For me it was much more than that. This was love at first sight, and I knew we were soul mates from a prior lifetime, and, most likely, from the one as Jesus.

I returned to Chicago. Back at Harlow's, I told Jimmy that since I had met the love of my life, I didn't need the club anymore. Jimmy was feeling burnt out and he, too, wanted to move on. So, we put the club up for sale and sold it instantly for the full asking price: lock, stock and barrel.

I felt a sense of completeness and peace. Once again, my life was about to change dramatically.

7: The Two Marriages

When I first met Elise at Harlow's I was very deep into the study of astrology and nothing could sidetrack me from my mission, not even Elise. Although I fell in love with her instantly, I knew what I needed to do to accomplish my spiritual mission, fulfill my spiritual destiny and fulfill my higher spiritual purpose.

The meta-science of astrology gave me a very deep understanding of my planetary energies in relation to how I presented myself to the world through my character, personality and individuality. We act in certain ways because of the energetic combination of the planets, their placement in the signs and constellations and their relation to other planets. A human being is a composite of the energies of the heavenly bodies. Those energies define who we are through our personality, character and individuality, but only as potentialities. We are the ones that create our outcomes. The trick is to master ones own self so the energies are impelling and not compelling. "Why Brutus, it is not in the stars but ourselves that we are underlings." William Shakespeare from Julius Caesar.

What I learned from astrology (and what fortified my belief that I was the reincarnation of Jesus) were the meanings of each of the astrological aspects in my horoscope chart. I read the book *Edgar Cayce On The Dead Sea Scrolls,* which said that Jesus studied astrology and that the *Essenes,* the mystical ascetic group that lived in Qumran by the Dead Sea in ancient Israel two thousand years ago, did astrological forecasts and predicted the coming of the messiah. So, I put two and two together. Jesus studied astrology. I studied astrology. What convinced me the most was the meaning of those planetary aspects, and I believed they could have easily been applied to Jesus.

I knew Jesus' destiny by heart, having read much of the *New Testament,* '*The Aquarian Gospel of Jesus the Christ'* by Levi, *'The Jesus Scroll'* by Donavon Joyce *'The Mystical Teachings of Jesus'* by Spencer and other esoteric books about Jesus. When I was born the planet Mercury was in my tenth house, indicating that destiny would require a show of eloquence from me because I have the ability to communicate with the public. I knew Jesus thrust himself into the public's eye when he began his ministry because it was his duty to intervene in the affairs of the world. This was Jesus' mission. I have the planet *Mars in my third house, which* means; "I will intervene in the world of public duties." It is an historical fact that Jesus stirred up dissent as he traveled around Israel to bring about needed spiritual changes. *Mars sextile Neptune* in my chart means; "I will stir up dissent to provoke necessary changes."

Every astrological description I read about myself I could easily apply to Jesus. The *Sun was in opposition to Neptune* when I was born and the astrology text said that means "I would direct my goals toward fulfilling some important responsibility." This was precisely Jesus' goal. It was his responsibility to fulfill the prophecies. This was the most important thing of all to him because it validated the scriptures, his role as messiah, that death was an illusion, confirmed God's existence, intelligent design, and plan for humanity.

We all know how Jesus selflessly helped others. *Venus was inconjunct to Jupiter* in my chart; "I will generously offer to serve the needs of others." I was connecting my past life to my present one, which made perfect sense to me. There was no delusional thinking; Jesus and I know who we are. I AM.

Jesus was a spiritual revolutionary and he constantly chastised and admonished the Jewish religious groups because they lived strictly by the letter of the law and not by the spirit of the law. He challenged them openly at every opportunity. He called them out on their hypocrisy and wickedness. I have *Mars sextile Uranus;* "I will challenge old ideas and doctrines that have outlived their usefulness." This is exactly what Jesus did, to the letter.

The Astrologer's Handbook and the computerized horoscope's meanings were convincing enough, although I lacked concrete 'proof' to directly link me to Jesus. The evidence from the astrological books was merely circumstantial and not enough to convince a jury, beyond a reasonable doubt. That is what I wanted: to eliminate any reasonable doubt. I would like cosmic justice. I would like to take reincarnation out of the category of just theory and put it in a class by itself: UNIVERSAL LAW based on the law of cause and effect karma. Jesus was, above all, a man of justice and when I learned I had S*un trine Saturn:* " just in my dealings with all men." I took it as one more affirmation of my past life as Jesus.

What Jesus wanted, and what all spiritual leaders want, is to make the world a better place. Everything Jesus did was for bringing light and truth and getting people to raise their sights and see with spiritual eyes, not just physical ones that see only the material. The material world, if not seen from a spiritual perspective is an illusion; it is not real. That illusion is darkness and even while standing in the brightest sunshine, one remains in abject darkness, completely and spiritually blind. When Jesus brought sight to the blind, it was not just a literal manifestation of someone being physically blind and then being able to see. When people come into the light, i.e. spiritual truth, and love, they are no longer blind. *Neptune trine the Descendant means:* "I will help to arouse every individual to use his or her highest values to make the world a better place to live." This described Jesus perfectly.

All of 1974 and 1975 was spent studying astrology and getting to know Elise and myself better. It was one and a half years since my encounter with God and I was on a mission, just like Jesus. With *Sun in my eleventh House*, I knew I had "a mission to accomplish" to re-create and re-member who I Am.

"I say to you that you are more holy and divine than you know; for even as I am of God and He is in me, so are you of God. First seek the kingdom and all powers shall be yours… draw in deeply from the mind which has brought forth creation and even now continues to guide all the stars. Wisdom is of God. In him are answers to all things. Therefore you must seek to **become One with Him** and all that you would know will be given unto you, even **the secret of the stars.**" (*The Lost Jesus Scroll* - Elizabeth MacGregor Burrows 2007, pp.107, 108).

By the time Elise returned from Tucson, I had already put the club up for sale and Tashandi and I began seeing Elise on a regular basis. She had her own dog named Tippy who disappeared one night while out walking with Elise's roommate's boyfriend. That was a 'tipping point' and the end of the roommate. Tippy somehow knew there was not enough space for two dogs and he sailed into the sunset. Although we looked at every animal shelter in the city, he was gone. Elise and Tippy had been together for fourteen years, so she gave in to her anger and resentment over his loss and it took her a long time to recover. Eventually she got over his disappearance. This was not a good way to start our relationship.

Elise's good friend Laura moved in with her and things settled down. I sold my house in Worth Woods, Illinois, and we spent more and more time at Elise's apartment. After Elise went to sleep I would pull all-nighters studying astrology and metaphysics. Elise thought something was wrong with me. She had just met me and this was not a side of me she had seen before. She liked the nightclub owner, and this version of me was too weird for her.

I did not share my big secret with her and knew I could not keep it hidden too much longer. Elise was Jewish and most Jews don't believe in Jesus and don't accept him as the 'promised' Messiah of the scriptures. How would she react when I divulged this potential relationship-killer? I figured if she really truly loved me she would accept me who I am as a person, and not who I thought I was in a past life.

One night I took Elise for dinner in Greek town, at *Dianna's Opah Restaurant*. Right before the flaming Saganaki cheese came out (after a couple of shots of Ouzo) I confessed. I told her I was Jesus in a past life. At that exact moment, the flaming Saganaki arrived at the table with the waiters' saying "Opah" and she dropped her jaw and her fork at the same time. She was in shock and didn't know what to say, so she said nothing at the restaurant.

On the way home Elise started screaming: "What do you mean you were Jesus? What are you talking about? Are you crazy? Who ARE you, anyway?" Elise's grandfather on her mother's side was an orthodox Rabbi and Jesus was considered a dirty word and was not welcome in their consciousness, let alone even being mentioned in their homes. Here was this guy she just met who owned a big nightclub, drove a Maserati, Lincoln Continental and thinks he was Jesus in a past life. Oy vey! What next? All those 'coincidences' were practically *Twilight Zone* material. If she didn't really love me she would have broken it off then and there. She knew deep down that I was credible and serious about my studies. I was not some deluded fanatic. It took many years before she actually accepted it. This does not mean she believed me. She trusted I knew what I was doing in relation to my research on the subject and went along with me.

By July of 1975, Tasha and I had moved in with Elise and there were quite a few arguments. After selling the club, I hadn't gone back to selling real estate yet. Elise was a professional model for the Playboy agency, so, with time on my hands, I drove her to her jobs. She entered beauty pageants, worked the trade shows, and posed for hundreds of modeling photographs. Elise was gorgeous, with a body to match. She was a true *Jewish American Princess.* And me? Well, I was the *Prince of Peace;* so, we were a good match.

Later that year, she introduced me to her former boyfriend, Steven Bernard, whose family manufactured dehydrated foods. I believed this was a great way to feed the hungry people of the world because it was non-perishable, easy to ship and relatively inexpensive. I called upon Reverend Tony at the *AME Church (African Methodist Episcopal)* in the *Cabrini Green* housing project, in one of the most dangerous parts of the city. I never considered any danger; I just wanted to present the program to feed the hungry. Unfortunately, Reverend Tony was no more interested in feeding the poor than the Pope was in converting to Judaism or Islam. The program fizzled and went nowhere.

That summer, I asked Elise to marry me (unofficially, as I didn't have a ring). She did not commit. That autumn I took her to Ocho Rios, Jamaica on our first trip together. We stayed at the *Tower Isle Hotel* where we met Lucien Chen who gave us a fully staffed villa to stay in for the week. The two of us together emitted such high energy attracting the rich and famous who showered favors on us. Together, we are a powerful combination.

My studies intensified and I read book after book on astrology, esoteric, and metaphysical subjects. I would fast for days at a time and run mile after mile to balance my spiritual life with my material life. Elise was definitely a girl of the world, and I was something else; somehow we stayed together, but just barely. The first year of our relationship was a real test. I was so in love with Elise my affections were too intense. Elise 'turned off,' which frustrated me and created a constant source of conflict. My studies must have really bothered her deep down.

Some of our fights were like Elizabeth Taylor's and Richard Burton's in *Who's Afraid Of Virginia Wolfe?* Epic. Once, Elise broke every piece of glassware in the china cabinet. I was not meeting her expectations. Her last boyfriend Steven was very rich, neither of them cooked, so they dined out nearly every meal. Steven took her to South America for three months and she was used to "la dolce vida" and expected nothing less from me. I really had to gear up financially.

Later that year, I proposed to Elise with the traditional diamond ring on bended knee. The limousine was waiting outside with both sets of parents and whisked us off to our engagement party at the brand new nightclub, *Zorine's* which opened that very same night. Elise and I were the first ones to dance on the clear glass dance floor. The *Chicago Tribune* was there to capture the moment, which made it into the celebrity column of the newspaper the following day. We planned the wedding for December 18, 1976, at the *Chicago Blackstone Hotel* on Michigan Avenue.

Before the end of the year another miracle happened. A woman lent me a book called *The Reappearance of the Christ* by Alice A. Bailey, published in 1948, the year of my birth. Was this another one of those amazing coincidences? Bailey said, "Someone is expected and his coming is anticipated… when the times are ripe he will come because it is universal law."

"Whenever there is a withering of the law and an uprising of lawlessness on all sides, then I manifest My-self. For the salvation of the righteous and the destruction of such as do evil, for the firm establishing of the Law, I come to birth age after age." *The Bhagavad Gita* Book IV, Sutra 7, 8.

Alice Bailey said that the Christ is someone who has a 'peculiar capacity (besides a self-initiated task and a preordained destiny) to transmit energy or divine power.' I knew from my chart and from studying the astrology texts that this book referred specifically to me because my astrology chart clearly indicated that very same "destiny" and "power."

One of my astrological aspects relating to the planet Uranus described me as a 'transmitting intermediary.' In other words, most of the descriptions for the 'coming' Christ as defined by Alice Bailey were the very same ones described in my horoscope. She referred to the **'magnetic will'** of Jesus. When I read that description, I noted in the side column in red ink the matching astrological aspect of *Mars sextile Neptune,* indicating 'strong personal **magnetism.**' She used the words 'mission' and 'destiny,' which were prominent in my chart. It all matched. After reading this book, there was no longer any doubt in my mind that I was the reincarnation of Jesus. However, I still lacked that critical evidence that would convince the world I was.

1976

On January 11, 1976, the attractive force was at work once again. My cousin, Irving Zimmerman, gave me several books to study. One was *Qabalism* by Dr. H.B. Pullen-Burry, published in 1925 by the *Yogi Publication Society*. In that book I learned that the 'King number is 10.' Qabala (which means to receive divine wisdom) introduced me to an even deeper spiritual reality; the world of numbers, the reincarnating soul, and the 'Law of Christ,' not the person, Jesus, but rather the energy frequency that represents the Love that is God that resides in every human being.

Spring came and Elise and I went to Puerto Vallarta, Mexico for a month. At a restaurant, we met Miki and Bennie Shapiro, who invited us to spend a few days at their villa in *Yelapa,* a two-hour speedboat ride away. There were no roads to *Yelapa*. Bennie and Miki said they were Bob Dylan's manager at the time. We all had great late night conversations about the world, music and esoterica. I brought with me a beautiful silk Chinese robe (back cover) which I wore around their house and with my long hair and beard, I looked, well, like Jesus. I used to perform many Bob Dylan songs in the '60's. What synchronicity to have met his managers! Bennie was also manager of *The Byrds* of *Turn, Turn, Turn* fame.

That autumn we drove the black Lincoln Mark III to Canada to see the changing of the leaves. Except for a few minor car problems (like the radiator springing a leak) the trip was exciting. We drove through Detroit, over to Windsor and on to Toronto, Montreal and Quebec. On the way back through Maine, we were searched by the Border Police. The black Lincoln (the car from the movie, *The French Connection*) my long hair and beard, portrayed me as a drug dealer. I had forgotten a small bag of pot in my pocket, which they found. "Look what we have here," the border agent exclaimed. Amazingly, they confiscated the pot and let us go. What a scare: the adrenaline was pumping hard, fast and furious.

December eighteenth was quickly approaching. It had been nearly three years since I had my close encounter with God and I still had no concrete evidence, other than looking like Jesus and being Jewish, to link me to this alleged past life. My horoscope indicated a mission to accomplish, a destiny to fulfill, and a plethora of other astrological aspects indicating world spiritual leadership. Even with *The Reappearance of the Christ* book published in the year of my birth, 1948, the book was not enough evidence to convince a jury beyond reasonable doubt that I was the reincarnation of Jesus.

For the past three years I was the ever-dedicated servant to God (does God need servants?), studying everything metaphysical, spiritual and mystical but no major breakthroughs to link the past life to the present one. All I was really going on was my intuition about this belief of mine, my faith, prayers, my studies, and the voice from God that confirmed it in 1973. For me this was not nearly enough. People who hear voices are not looked upon too kindly in society and I was not some crazy, delusional person doing drugs. I was a very successful real estate broker who owned property, a night club, cars and all kinds of material stuff; the stuff that makes someone a respected member of society, superficial as it all is, and I was going to do the material world thing of getting married. It was the Rabbi thing to do.

Just five days before the big wedding I mysteriously came into possession of a book called *The Passover Plot* by Dr. Hugh Schonfield, an eminently and internationally renowned Jewish scholar and author of *The Authentic New Testament*. *The Passover Plot* was first published in England in 1965, the same year I graduated from *Evergreen Park High School*. In this book I found the hidden treasure I had been seeking to find: the missing link, the Holy Grail, the lost key, the mother lode, the full monte.

It took Dr. Schonfield forty years to paint a full personality portrait of Jesus. I finally had the hard evidence that could link incontrovertibly the past life as Jesus to my present lifetime. The discovery was beyond belief, but the hard evidence was there. Bear in mind, in 1974 I studied *The Astrologer's Handbook* and the computerized horoscope programmed from the book *Planets in Aspect* by Robert Pelletier published in 1973, the very same year of my *Close Encounter of the God Kind*, so, I was ready for what I discovered in *The Passover Plot*.

As I began reading the book I started recognizing familiar words and paragraphs that were in the astrology books. Could this be possible? Identical descriptions of Jesus and myself? Did Dr. Schonfield collaborate with the authors of those astrology books I studied? I quickly ruled that out. Ten years separated those texts. Yet, remarkably, the comparisons were strikingly similar. As I read *The Passover Plot* I underlined nearly every word and paragraph. Everything matched. It was just like reading *The Reappearance of the Christ*.

A paragraph from the P*assover Plot* that was most stunning was when Dr. Schonfield said of Jesus: "What is so striking in the gospels as scholars have noted is the dynamic purposefulness of Jesus. He **proceeds methodically** to carry out certain actions calculated to have particular effects and leading up to a predetermined conclusion. It is as if he were a chemist in a laboratory, confidently following a formula set down in an authoritative textbook. There is scarcely a hint of hesitation or indecision. He is like a **Chess-Player** with a master plan who has anticipated and knows how to counter the moves of his opponent and indeed to make them serve the ends of his design."

The words that are **bolded** are what I underlined in the book or highlighted with a marker. All these personality descriptions and a hundred and fifteen more nearly identical comparisons are also presented in *My Past Life As Jesus-An Autobiography of Two Lifetimes* and *Messiah For Hire-The Reincarnation of Jesus?* So, after I read this paragraph in the *Passover Plot,* I searched for the astrological aspect that matched it in the computerized horoscope or *Astrologer's Handbook.* I found it. It was *Saturn sextile the ascendant.* Here's what it means. (Bruce) '**plans methodically** before doing anything. Because he understands people so well he can be effective in positions of leadership matching the right person with the proper role as cleverly as a **Chess-Player**.'

Dr. Schonfield says Jesus '*proceeds methodically*.'

Saturn sextile the ascendant says I '*plan methodically*.'

Dr. Schonfield described Jesus in 1965 '<u>like</u> a **Chess-Player'**, and ten years later, in 1975, I am described '<u>as</u> a **Chess-Player'**. Twenty years later, in 1995, Laurie Beth Jones in her book, *Jesus CEO,* described Jesus as 'an **effective leader**.' Compare this to *Saturn sextile Neptune* that describes me as '**effective in positions of leadership**.' Is this merely coincidence?

Jesus CEO: '*An effective leader*'.

Saturn sextile Neptune: '*effective in positions of leadership*'.

Do you see any discernible difference between the two descriptions? For now, just rule it coincidence and leave it at that.

As you will soon see, this **pattern** of near identical descriptions occurs over one hundred twenty-five times (actually one hundred seventy-five, but I stopped comparing at one hundred twenty-five), so you will need to ask yourself this question at some point in this book: Is this **identical pattern** of the two personalities the result of a deliberate and genuine hidden structure, part of the intelligent design of God (for lack of better words) that I discovered, just as Einstein discovered the theory of relativity? Is it part of an encoded message from the great unknown we call God, the Unity, Oneness, the infinite universe?

In the science of cryptology, this is a crucial question. If someone can determine how unlikely a given pattern can arise by chance then we have our answer as to how likely it is that the **structure of the pattern** is deliberate and not by chance. In other words, in the chapter on the numbers in my book *My Past Life As Jesus – An Autobiography of Two Lifetimes (*2001), we see the very same pattern emerge with the number ten (10), the King number. How unlikely is it then that there are over one hundred and fifty occurrences of the number ten in the universal framework? You got a glimpse of this numerological pattern in *The Prologue*. Where does amazing coincidence stop? At what point? And when do you begin confirming that the pattern is deliberate? At what point? If you ask this question you differentiate the pre-scientific approach from the scientific approach to the investigation. From *Cracking the Bible Code* by Dr. Jeffrey Satinover. And that is what this book is about; an investigation into **the patterns of the reincarnating soul** presented scientifically through many different scientific applications as well as the metaphysical ones.

How unlikely is it then that there are 125 pattern matches between the personalities of Jesus and myself? Also, how unlikely is it that I made this discovery to begin with? If you decide that it is totally unlikely, i.e. beyond amazing coincidence, then it is totally likely that **the patterning is deliberate**. But, by whom? Or, by what? The critical scientific measure to determine in this book is: which one is correct? "It isn't **how the pattern occurs** or **how often we expect the pattern to occur** on theoretical grounds, i.e. in scientific jargon, the expectation value of its occurrence, but both of these combined as the important measure." Dr. Satinover.

As you read this book ask yourself the above questions. **Is the hidden structure of the pattern deliberate** intended by God, the universal all-in-all? Is it genuine or did I manipulate the information in order to trick and fool you? (Only a fool would do that!) And then, ask yourself the question as you read the book. Do the statistical probabilities, i.e. likely as opposed to unlikely, of the patterning support the evidence that the soul that inhabited the body of Jesus now inhabits my body? You will be the judge and jury of this and, if you can keep an open mind, then it may lead you to some hitherto unknown truth that your soul needs for its own re-creation process in the re-membering of who *you* are. Then you can write your own future incarnation by your thoughts if you make the choice to reincarnate.

"Sometimes a new reality forces itself to be recognized and then things can shift. **New patterns of intelligence arise** and **then a deep transformation can take place**." *Wrinkles In Time* by physicist George Smoot-1994: pp. 291, 296.

"Cryptology or cryptanalysis is the procedure to translate or interpret secret writings, as **codes** and **ciphers,** for which the **key** is unknown." *Webster's New Universal Unabridged Dictionary* - 1996. I have the "cipher" to the encoded message. I have the "key." We all have the key. It's inside of us waiting to be discovered. *"Love Is The Key"* (song by Bruce) that unlocks the door to the "kingdom of God."

When I began matching the personality of Jesus to my own personality portrait you can understand my excitement and amazement. This was right before my marriage to this amazing woman *Elise.* Now that the spiritual marriage had been consummated, I was ready for her, and a challenge far greater and more difficult than verifying my past life as Jesus which was a walk in the park.

It was over sixty degrees fahrenheit on December 18, 1976. The sun was shining and the sky was bright blue. Sally, Elise's mom, put together a beautiful wedding. All of our friends were there as well, the relatives from both sides of the family. Even some people neither of us knew were there. There were three bands that played so there was no shortage of entertainment. There was an all black soul band, the *Lou Conti Orchestra* and my own rock band. Not *The King James Version* but a new later version with new members.

Three of the bridesmaids fainted at the same time: Bonnie, Laura and Cindy. What a scene! One fell, then another and then another all lying on the carpet in crumpled piles. It wasn't hot inside or anything they had eaten (we hadn't eaten yet), they just fell like dominos.

After everyone recovered and were back on their feet, Jim Dorchak (my friend from 1972) played *'Stairway to Heaven'* by Led Zeppelin as Elise and I each marched down the aisle; I was with my mom and Elise with her dad. Everybody had a wonderful time. When it came time for the champagne toast Elise presented me with a solid gold Aum necklace (back cover). When I worked at India Gifts and Foods on Belmont Ave in the 60's I bought an Aum made out of brass. Aum is the East Indian mystical symbol for peace, love, eternal life, universality, unity and oneness. It is the sound one makes when sitting in a lotus position with legs crossed, eyes closed and meditating on... God. Aum, Aum, Aummmmmmmmmmm. Elise took the brass one to a goldsmith who replicated it in solid gold. What a surprise! It was her way of saying, "I support you and I am there with you in your spiritual journey." She had absolutely no idea what she was getting herself into. Neither did I.

The following day, we checked into the *MGM Grand Hotel* in Las Vegas, where I recognized the roaring MGM lion as the symbolic *Lion of Judah.* Jesus was known as the *Lion of Judah.* Elise came down with some unknown illness and the honeymoon was not all that sweet. Ours was a very old 'karmic' relationship and not our first attempt at marriage by any means. *The Dead Sea Scrolls* reveal our unresolved issues from past lives. What those issues are can be found in the books, *Jesus the Man and Jesus and the Riddle of the Dead Sea Scrolls* by Barbara Thiering.

1977 would prove to be another momentous year.

December 18, 1976

8: The Ernest Digweed Estate, Halloween, The Worst Winter

Now that Elise and I were married it was time to find a new home. I was selling real estate again with a new company I opened with three other partners. We called it Americorp and I began making good money like I always had in real estate. 1977 was a boom year for me.

In the Chicago Tribune I saw an ad for a one-bedroom sublet at *Lake Point Tower* on the 57th floor. *Lake Point Tower* was the same building that astrologer Laurie Brady lived in when I had my astrological reading in 1975. I decided this is where we were going to live. The sublet had been rented by the time I got there so I went down to the rental office on the second floor. Miraculously, a two-bedroom 2-bath 28th floor corner apartment with full city and lake views become available that morning. I rented it on the spot. The huge column in the living room was already mirrored in amber glass and the apartment was the perfect size for the two of us, Tashandi, and the cats, Zuma and Mama Tasha.

The rent was much more than my budget would allow, but "where there is a will there is a way." With the Maserati and the black Lincoln Mark III, we looked like Hollywood elite, but it was a monthly challenge to pay for this kind of lifestyle. Despite this apparent contradiction to my spiritual beliefs, I understood completely that the material world was just an illusion. My rising sign (the sign that was ascending at the time of my birth) was Taurus (in the sidereal system) and I projected an image of materiality. This was a classic case of *Clark Kent* and *Superman*. What you see is not always what you get.

Lake Point Tower is at 505 North Lake Shore Drive, off Grand Avenue. With *Navy Pier* right behind, Lake Point Tower was the only high-rise building east of Lake Shore Drive. The building looked directly at the entire city skyline, as it stood majestically all by itself. It was also the world's tallest residential building (seventy-three stories) inspired by famed architect Mies van der Rohe. From an aerial view, it looked like a four-leaf clover. It had an outdoor two and a half acre wooded park with duck pond, waterfalls, swimming pool and recreation area on the third floor. The second floor featured a supermarket, health club, shops, boutiques, offices and a spectacular supper club on the 73rd floor.

The apartment was nicely appointed with no flooring, no drapes, no furniture, nothing; just appliances. I had to build it. I put Mexican paver tiles in the foyer and kitchen floors, colorful hand painted blue and yellow Mexican ceramic tiles on the lower half of the kitchen walls. Vinyl wall covering in the foyer that resembled an ancient temple, wood parquet in the second bedroom and plush cream colored wall-to-wall carpeting throughout the living room, hallway and master bedroom.

Elise's uncle Sol was in the drapery business and gave us a great deal on the see-through pull-down sun-shades and sheer drapes that needed electric motors to drive the vast expanse of windows in the living and dining rooms. I bought two sectional couches from the sublet on the 57th floor and filled the rest of the apartment with my Mexican furniture from *Pier One Imports*.

As an additional surprise for Elise, I hired Fred Sperry (the artist that did the art-work for *Harlow's*) to paint a four-by-six-foot portrait of Elise (from one of her more provocative modeling photos) to hang on the wall in the living room. I also bought her a baby grand piano, which my mother found advertised in the newspaper. The piano's owner practiced mysticism and past life regression. I agreed to a session. As the three of us sat in a circle holding hands, the man went into a hypnotic trance and began breathing very deeply. After several very long minutes, he said he saw me with a beard and long hair, carrying something very heavy on my back, but could see nothing else. Neither my mom or I said anything about Jesus to him. He was a stranger with whom we had no prior contact. It was just another affirmation, totally unscientific, in the realm of amazing coincidence.

After the construction was completed and the decor installed, it was time for Elise to see the apartment. The phone company assigned to us the number 644-3470.

Apartment 2811 at Lake Point Tower

That summer, we became friends with Aaron Gold, the celebrity columnist for the *Chicago Tribune*. The movie *Grease*, starring John Travolta and Olivia Newton-John was going to premier in Chicago and Aaron invited us to the movie and gala party. Her song from *Xanadu* said, "**you have to believe we are magic**...planets align so rare." I was born when the planets Saturn and Pluto were in conjunction, which means the '**aspect of the magician**.' Elise and I are a powerful combination and we attracted whatever we needed into our lives.

One day, at breakfast, Elise read me an article from the *Chicago Tribune*: "Ernest Digweed, a retired teacher from Portsmouth, England died (in 1976) and left his entire estate of approximately $44,000 to Jesus 'Christ' on the occasion of His return to the earth. In order to claim the estate, the will stated, Christ must return specifically to 'reign on earth' and must prove his identity to the British Government."

In another article, "Digweed instructed the *Office of the Public Trustee* to invest his money in government bonds, guaranteeing Jesus a total yield of $615,800 by the end of the 20th century. Digweed's heirs are contesting the will and have offered an unusual solution: an insurance policy in the same amount payable to Jesus upon his return. Since then, another problem has cropped up. Two individuals, each insisting that he is Jesus reborn, have filed claims for the money."

This was an opportunity that would allow me to satisfy the requirements of the Digweed estate. I wasn't interested in 'reigning on earth,' but I did want to 'prove my identity before the British Government.' After reading *The Passover Plot* by Dr. Hugh Schonfield, matching my astrological chart to the personality descriptions of Jesus in the book, plus calculating the numerological sequencing of the number 10 and specifically the number 28, I believed I was ready to go to London and meet with th*e Office of the Public Trustee.* I wrote them a letter and they responded as follows:

DY/JL

PUBLIC TRUSTEE OFFICE

Reference: G8074/N5

Kingsway, London WC2B 6 JX

E N Digweed DECEASED G8074/N5

21 September 1977

Dear Mr. Travis

I am in receipt of your letter of 10 September addressed to Mr. Beecham as the administration of this case is dealt with by this writer.

You will appreciate that the Public Trustee has received several hundred letters from people all over the world who claim to be entitled to the late Mr. Digweed's estate and offer to prove their identity.

It is not possible for the Public Trustee to enter into correspondence with or grant interviews to all of these people and no exceptions can be made.

This matter has been referred for legal advice and it is now for the Court to decide the way in which the Public Trustee should proceed.

No further information is available for release.

Yours sincerely,

Miss D Young

ON HER MAJESTY'S SERVICE

Mr. B R Travis

505 N. Lake Shore Dr.

Apartment 2811

Chicago, Illinois, USA

No sooner had the letter arrived that Elise and I made plans to travel to London, meet with the *Office of the Public Trustee* and claim the estate of Ernest Digweed. 1977 was the year of the *Queen's Silver Jubilee* and the city exuded a festive atmosphere. We stayed at The *Blake's Hotel* in South Kensington and each day we would walk past *Harrod's Department Store* and into the city. We went to plays, a medieval banquet, experienced the play *As You Like It* by William Shakespeare at Stratford On Avon, toured Oxford University and did the American tourist in London thing.

One morning, I called the *Office of the Public Trustee* and explained I was in London from Chicago and would like to come in and discuss the estate of Ernest Digweed. It was just one year after Mr. Digweed had passed away and his bequest was still a very hot topic in England. A time was set and I took the subway (called the 'tube') to get there. The Trustee building looked like the weather; grey and gloomy. I approached the receptionist' desk, gave my name and was told to take a seat. There were two very old gentlemen within earshot of the desk and I overheard them say, "That's the guy who thinks he's Jesus." They were expecting me.

After a twenty-minute wait, Mr. Beecham came to meet with me right in the lobby. He was not going to waste his time by taking me to his office. Another crackpot! It was pouring rain now and he proceeded to ask me whether I could walk on water, bring sight to the blind, perform miracles and healings. Understandably, the meeting was adversarial on his part and there was no way to respond to his perfectly legitimate questions other than quoting Jesus so I said to him: "Unless you see signs and miracles you won't believe?" I was Jewish, had very long hair and a beard and for all intents and purposes I looked the part. Of all the hundreds of people attempting to claim the estate, how many were Jewish and looked like Jesus? And, how many made the pilgrimage to London? Undaunted, I left even more full of conviction and determination. I knew who I had been in a past life and I was not going to let this rejection set me back. Albert Einstein said, "Great spirits have always encountered violent opposition from mediocre minds." The 'opposition' would prove to be very intense for the next thirty-eight years and most anyone exposed to my 'belief' would stand in judgment without even examining the hard evidence.

In 967 B.C.E., King Solomon, son of King David said, "He that answereth a matter before he heareth it, it is folly and shame unto him." *Proverbs 18:13*. The way to avoid this pitfall is to 'keep an open mind.' In 1725, in Southampton, England, Isaac Watts, the greatest living preacher of his time said, "Search for evidence of truth with diligence and honesty, and be heartily ready to receive evidence, whether for the agreement or disagreement of ideas. Do not indulge yourself to wish any unexamined proposition were true or false. A wish often perverts the judgment and tempts the mind strangely to believe upon slight evidence whatsoever we wish to be true or false."

Back in Chicago, Halloween was just days away and *Faces Nightclub* on Rush Street was having a big costume party. Elise and I were members, so I seized on this as the perfect opportunity to recreate the crucifixion of Jesus. I wore a loincloth, a simulated crown of thorns with fake blood flowing down over my forehead and my back to recreate the lashings (photos in *My Past Life As Jesus*). That night singer Tom Jones was there dressed all in black with a big crucifix around his neck. I went up to Tom and said,

"Bless you my son." I was only twenty-nine years old at the time but fully consciously aware of the drama life is in the 3D material world.

I was picked to be one of the five qualifiers in the costume contest. Next to me facing the judges was famed socialite, Beverly Crown who also lived at *Lake Point Tower.* While the contestants were being judged, I told Beverly I was just acting out my past life as Jesus and just being myself. She called me Jesus the entire night. Her husband Barry was a skeptic (most Jews do not accept Jesus) and refused to take me seriously. However, Beverly seemed to understand and accept the concept of reincarnation. Elise and I were invited into their close circle of family and friends. We socialized, dined together and met in faraway places when we traveled: St. Tropez, Miami, Aspen and eventually, Maui, where Elise and I would take up part time residence in 1979. The Law of Attraction was at work in all its manifestation in the material world.

December came and with it one of the worst winters in Chicago's history with sub-zero temperatures for thirty days in a row. I had to wrap Tasha's feet when I walked her. We left Chicago the following December after sub-letting our apartment and moved to Maui for the winter. We would never spend another winter in Chicago again.

HATFIELD HOUSE
LONDON, ENGLAND

1977

9: Telling The Story [1978 to 1981]

By 1978 I focused on getting this reincarnational information out to the media. Ron Hunter, the evening anchor on *NBC News*, lived at *Lake Point Tower*. I made it a point to introduce myself to him and we became acquainted. I wrote letters to Aaron Gold, who was sympathetic to my cause and he wished me well in my endeavor for world peace. Although Ron and Aaron probably thought I was crazy, they treated me with respect and gave me some of their time. I wrote each of them letters divulging "secret" information.

I truly believed I was the reincarnation of Jesus and felt compelled to get this discovery out to the world. Little did I know I would still be trying to do exactly that in 2015, forty-two years after my close encounter with God in 1973. This was truly 'ignorance is bliss,' as it never occurred to me that God decided the moment for me to gain recognition for this work. Only God knoweth the hour. *Matthew 24:36.*

1978 was a year of traveling from downtown Chicago to the southwest side where my real estate office was located at 79th and Pulaski. Business was good and I was still deep into my studies. Many books about the mystical Jesus and the 'Christ vibration' came my way and I learned more and more about the nature of reality and my true self. I took copious notes on everything I read networking all the complex information in my mind.

Don and Bobbi, the neighbors from *Lake Point Tower* with the sublet were now living in Kaneohe, Hawaii on the island of Oahu. They insisted we come and visit. After the winter of 1977 we were ready. I made arrangements to study for the Hawaii real estate exam so we could go back to Maui in the winters. By December, Chicago already had two big snowstorms and the conditions were dismal. We sublet our apartment for four months and some friends agreed to take care of Tashandi and the cats. We left with some peace of mind.

Three weeks on Oahu was just enough. New Year's Eve in Waikiki was quite the happening. On January 1st, I left for Maui. Elise was offered a swimsuit modeling job on the beach at the lagoon at the *Hilton Hawaiian Village*. That night Elise called hysterically. The photographer's assistant told her to take off her jewelry and put it in a bag for safekeeping. After the photo shoot she discovered her wedding ring was missing. She hired someone to scan the beach with a metal detector with no results. The woman assigned to hold her jewelry later became a newscaster for one of the local television stations and every time Elise saw her on television it brought back a very bad memory. To this day we have no idea how the ring disappeared. It will always be a mystery. Elise's first day on Maui was January 2, 1979. She was so emotionally distraught she shredded every piece of paper in the condominium and covered the floor wall to wall. It would be years before I could replace a ring as special as that one. The condominium we rented went up for sale so we bought it. A lot more expensive than a ring.

I bought an old green *Fiat X-19* convertible and we had many happy driving trips to Lahaina under the stars. We went to *Charlie Young Beach* at *Kamaole Beach 1* every day, where I studied for the exam enjoying the laid back Maui lifestyle.

One of the very first persons we met was Drake. There was an immediate attraction. It turned out we both had read the *Urantia* book. The *Urantia* book, Part IV, recounts the Life and Teachings of Jesus and the instructions given to Jesus by the angelic being Michael before Jesus reincarnated. According to the book, Jesus understood that his re-incarnation was completely voluntary and that as a mere mortal, he relinquished his celestial attributes and powers (at birth) but that 'he could reinstate himself with full power and authority at any time.' This was part of his re-creation and re-membering process.

The purpose of incarnation according to the book was for Jesus to experience 'perfected human understanding.' The evidence of the reinstatement of this **power and authority** of Jesus in this present incarnation is revealed by the *Sun trine Pluto* which means that I am 'qualified to gain positions of **power and authority** with tremendous power and will.'

In the living of Jesus' earth life, he would become progressively self-conscious regarding his divine mission in a human flesh body. The *Urantia* book described Jesus as a blend of his parents' dispositions many of which manifest in my present lifetime: 'Unusual gentleness, **courageous,** sunny disposition, conscientious, sympathetic understanding, tremendous capacity for **righteous indignation**, optimistic, **determined,** et al.' With *Sun trine Pluto* my 'attitude is one of **righteous indignation** towards those who attempt to bend the truth or take liberties with the law.' This aspect described me as '**courageous and determined.**'

Urantia Book | Jesus: Power and Authority

Sun Trine Pluto | Bruce: Power and Authority

Urantia Book | Jesus: Righteous Indignation

Sun Trine Pluto | Bruce: Righteous Indignation

Urantia Book | Jesus: Courageous and Determined

Sun Trine Pluto | Bruce: Courageous and Determined

Coincidence?

Drake and I hit it off immediately. Was it a coincidence that Drake was also born on April 2nd and that he studied the *Urantia* Book? Maui was doing its magic already and I recognized all the synchronistic clues. "The more we learn, the more we see how it all fits together; how there is an underlying unity to the sea of matter and stars and galaxies that surround us. Is this then where scientific explanation breaks down and God takes over?" *The Mind of God* by physicist Paul Davies.

The Blue Max was the nightspot for name entertainment in Lahaina and Longhi's was the most popular restaurant. Bob Longhi was quite a character. He was into astrology, numerology and everything esoteric. We became acquainted and friendly sharing past life theories. Bob would not comment one-way or the other about my past life beliefs.

In April I took the real estate sales person's exam and we returned to Chicago and our apartment at *Lake Point Tower.* That summer, Pope John Paul II came to Chicago and I could see the crowds from our living room windows on the 28th floor. Is it just a coincidence that Pope John Paul II died on the day of my birth, April 2nd? Is it a coincidence that the movie the *Matrix* was released on April 2nd? Is it a coincidence that two of the four-tetrad blood moon cycles were on April 2nd?

1980 was another important year of learning for me. I studied the book *Reincarnation-An East West Anthology* by Head and Cranston and discovered the early church fathers, *St. Clement of Alexandria, Origin, St. Gregory, St. Jerome, St. Augustine, Synesius* and others taught reincarnation. I learned that the ancient Jews were continually expecting the reincarnation of their great prophets and that karma is connected to the law of re-birth or the re-incarnation of the same spiritual individuality in a series of personalities. I knew these principles intuitively and always appreciated the affirmations.

In the 4th century, the Roman emperor Constantine took over the rule of the fledgling Christian church. At the *Council of Nicea* in 325 A.D. the teachings of reincarnation were made anathema and heretical to its own doctrine of confession and intercession by priests. Teaching reincarnation back then could result in being put to death. With reincarnation now considered taboo only the church could give the soul a second chance. The church seized control and turned a pure teaching into big business. To this day reincarnation is anathema to the church and Christianity and anyone who believes in it is still considered a heretic 1800 years later.

Elise and I returned to Maui in January 1980 and I began selling real estate for *Kamaole Realty.* My office was right across the street from Kamaole Beaches 1 & 2 at Kihei Kai Nani Village. On my very first day after work I walked across the street to where Elise was on the beach. I was very excited and animated about real estate on Maui and talking quite loudly. As we were leaving an older couple stopped us. The husband overheard my conversation with Elise and said he had been unsuccessful in finding vacant oceanfront property they could invest in. I told him I would find him the perfect property. Three days later I made my first sale. I sold them **28** oceanfront acres for $350K! This property was not listed in the MLS (multiple listing service). I did a lot of research and found it. We needed transportation so I bought the perfect Maui sports car. A Jeep C-J 5 Wolfpack in bright yellow with wide bands of orange and black pinstripes going over the hood. A photo of this very same jeep with Elise and I in it went global. We sold the Fiat X-19 before we left Maui the year before.

In February, a 100-year storm wiped out most of the beaches and gold hit $850.00 per ounce. We rented a cottage in *Maui Meadows,* replete with scorpions and centipedes. It only took a few days for Elise to say enough. We found a one-bedroom two-bath ocean view condominium at the new Wailea Ekolu Village in Wailea Resort. Shortly after we moved in it went on the market for sale. We made an offer, which was accepted. The market was going crazy.

Everything was going up and up and Elise insisted we purchase the Wailea condominium. We sold the condo we bought the year before and a few months later the real estate market crashed. We got out of that one in the nick of time but got stuck with the Wailea condominium at a big price. I put all my cash into it and over extended myself.

The real estate market was crashing and we returned to Chicago in a financial panic. Overnight our equity in the condominium disappeared and there was no market to sell it. We found a long-term tenant and covered our mortgage. We were back in our *Lake Point Tower* apartment with no money. Real estate wasn't profitable right away, so I cut my hair short shaved off my beard and tried selling insurance. What a disaster! I got very depressed. A small loan from my parents allowed me to start selling houses again and get back on my feet. It was very scary and very humbling: I tied up all my money and left myself vulnerable. This turned out to be another major blessing in disguise.

That summer *Lake Point Tower* threw a big party for the residents on the third floor and the theme was a Hawaiian luau. We invited our friends Paul and Valeta Rice from Maui to visit and be our guests. They were master numerologists and authors of the book *Triadic Communication*. The flower leis were of the plastic variety but the party was memorable. Everyone knew Elise and I were spending our winters on Maui and we were featured in the *Lake Point Tower* newsletter, playing the part of the "Life styles of the rich and famous." Even Tashandi was in the spotlight for a *Fendi* fur fashion show and was picked up in a limousine. The *Bonwit Teller* fur salon sponsored the event. Besides paying her a decent wage they made her a fur coat and collar: pure decadence. She even made it into the celebrity section of the Chicago Tribune. One never would have guessed I had been Jesus in a past life. Jesus? Driving a Maserati and a Lincoln Continental? Living in a high-rise apartment on Lake Shore Drive? Socializing with the Crowns. A platinum blond Afghan hound dog. Are you kidding me? No way!!! Impossible!!

There is an astrological explanation to this seemingly extreme material lifestyle. It has to do with the pre-natal solar and lunar eclipses (sidereal) before my birth in November 1947. According to Spiller and McCoy in their book *Spiritual Astrology-Your Personal Path to Self-Fulfillment p. 187 (1985)* "My lesson is to develop a proper prosperity consciousness in this lifetime. I am coming from a previous existence that was extremely spiritual but materially poverty stricken. I took a vow of poverty in a past incarnation in order to focus my energy on my spiritual development...I am here to learn that when I allow my spirituality to manifest through good works that support my fellow human beings, money is a natural by-product of that service; money is simply another aspect of life that needs to be mastered."

In 2005 Karen McCoy did a past life regression for me and confirmed I was Jesus in a past life. She taped the entire session but refused to release it to me because she felt it would jeopardize her privacy. To this day she refuses to release it. It makes no matter.

She sent me a signed copy of her book that said: "Dear Bruce, Many blessings on your spiritual journey. Love and Light. Karen."

In December, we traded our Wailea condominium for a house in Aspen. During a big snowstorm, the announcement came on the radio that John Lennon had been murdered in front of the *Dakota* apartment building in New York City. John was a spiritual visionary with mystical leanings having spent time in India with *Maharishi Mahesh Yogi*. John captured the essence of the meaning of life with the song, "*All You Need Is Love*. Love is all you need. LOVE, LOVE, LOVE. ALL YOU NEED IS LOVE." How much simpler can a message be? John knew the truth and his murder was not a freak accident. It was a result of some past life karmic interaction with his killer. "For everything there is a season, and a time for every purpose under heaven; a time to be born and a time to die.' *Ecclesiastes 3:1-2. Turn Turn Turn.*

1980 was another eventful year in Chicago, which was filled with excitement. However, it was time once again to return to Maui. This time we sublet our apartment for a much longer period. We had to bring the two cats and Tasha to Maui as they were getting older and being apart from them for so long was very distressing for them and for us.

Hawaii imposed a four-month quarantine so we conjured up all kinds of ways to smuggle the animals in. We slightly sedated the cats and brought them on board the plane with us. There was no smuggling a big dog. Tasha was relegated to the cargo section. When we arrived on Oahu we were required to go to the quarantine facility where Tasha was to remain for four months. We followed the van that transported her to the site. It was blazing hot. We checked her in, filled out the paperwork and followed the worker to her outdoor cage. After saying our good-byes we flew back to Maui. Five days later, we received a call from the quarantine station: 'Your dog is dying; you'd better come over now and claim her.' I flew over immediately. Tasha had gone on a hunger strike protesting her abhorrent conditions; her long platinum locks were matted, and she was a mess. She came to life the moment our eyes met.

I moved her to the *Care Animal Hospital on* Kapahulu near *Diamond Head Park*. The facility was indoors, air conditioned, piped in music, top quality food and Tasha was walked three times a day. I put pictures of Elise and me on her walls and made her very comfortable. Tasha was saved in the nick of time. The universe was looking out for us.

I flew back and forth nearly every week to visit Tasha to keep her company. I would stay with her all day until the clinic closed at 8:00 at night. I really loved her.

Four months flew by (probably not for Tasha) and it was time for her to come home. Elise remained on Maui waiting at the airport for us to arrive. With a real flower lei greeting and a photographer from the Maui News Tasha was all smiles. The newspaper gave her a half page picture and a big story of what happened in her life. Her arrival on Maui was a little bit better than Elise's two years before.

1981 was a momentous year numerologically and is explained in the chapter on the numbers in *My Past Life As Jesus-An Autobiography of Two Lifetimes (2001)*. Passover and Easter were on the same weekend, (as was in 2015) and we went to Hana, Maui, to conduct a Seder (Jewish Passover service) on Hamoa Beach. I had never performed such a service before (in this lifetime). It required a Haggadah, which was the religious manual on how to conduct the ceremony. Elise had arranged to have one flown from Honolulu to the tiny Hana airport and miraculously it was delivered on time. At the same time the Haggadah was delivered it had gotten dark and we could not find a light switch anywhere in the pavilion. All of a sudden the lights in the facility came on automatically. 'Let there be light.' The timing was sensational. Everyone was in awe at the events and there could be no doubt that God was present and choreographing the whole movie.

On the back cover of the Haggadah, next to the price, was the number 28. Coincidence? We rented an apartment at the Aloha Cottages, which at that time had a 28-mile marker sign in front. Even the phone number for the cottages added up to a 28. It was a very mystical weekend, with special spiritual importance, as 1981 was the inverse and a permutation of 1918 and 1891, all critically important years in the numerological patterning spoken of in *The Prologue* and all adding up to the number 19, (1 + 9 = 10 = 1 + 0 = 1) the number of the Alpha and Omega (also spoken of in the *Book of Revelation 1:8)*.

The night of the Seder some native Hawaiians put out their nets in the bay to catch fish. In the morning, I was invited to retrieve the nets but there was only one fish. That Easter Sunday afternoon, we went horseback riding and I was given a white horse: the white horse from the New Testament *Book of Revelation 6:2*. 1981 was also the year of *Birkat Hachama,* the blessing of the sun and a very auspicious time in the Jewish calendar occurring every 28 years.

Later that year, *The Onearth Gathering,* a spiritual event sponsored by Bruce and Eileen Cady of the *Findhorn Foundation* in Sweden, was held in Kihei at the *Mana Kai* condominium. Eileen Cady was a psychic and she told me in her reading that I was on the 'Jesus ray of energy.' We met a girl who claimed to have an alien connection, as in outer space alien, who had a dream about someone with a yellow Jeep. She did not know I had a yellow Jeep.

The three of us stayed up all night in our condominium watching the moon rise over Haleakala and sink into the ocean. During the night we all noticed a red light bouncing around in the kitchen. We immediately got up from the couch and ran over to see a small illuminated glowing round ball, dancing around and bouncing off the walls and the cabinets. Then, all of a sudden, it went through the wall and skipped over the rooftop of a building below. Was this some form of alien visitation?

By 1981, the poetic messages that I had been receiving since 1966 had all but ceased. The more I studied and learned, the less frequent the transmissions. My studies were as intense as ever, and I was reading volume after volume of esoteric books. By the end of the year I began studying for the Hawaii real estate broker's license because I wanted to open up my own office. I was making too much money for *Kamaole Realty* and they were not willing to give me the percentage split I wanted so I made preparations to move on. The high point of the year was running the 26.2 mile Maui Marathon, which I finished in 5 hours and 5 minutes. The race number assigned to me was 901.

10: MY Fate is Sealed [1982 to 1984]

1982 was the last year I received a message from the cosmos. It was cryptic.

"The story wasn't exciting enough."

This is the last poem of *Messiah For Hire-Poems From Inner Space 1966-1982*. They completely stopped. I studied biblical prophecy in depth and I was feeling more confident about my past life beliefs more than ever before. I went to the television stations in Chicago with my story, wrote letters to news anchors and reporters, and did everything in my power to make something happen regarding my discovery. The truth is no one cared. Reincarnation and past lives were still taboo. Once in a while an article would surface in the newspaper about someone on the other side of the world who had a vivid past life experience, but it was rare. I still foolishly thought it was within my power to help change the world. It was, except it was light years away. You cannot force something of this magnitude upon humanity. The time had already been determined in God's intelligent design and whenever that time was by that I must abide.

In 1981, I started writing letters to the Maui News. On December 7th (my mother's birthday) they printed my letter on the meaning of the word Christ and what Christ-mas really meant. I slipped my message to the world just in time, in the great cosmic year of 1981.

On April 11, 1982, I wrote a lengthy letter (condensed) as follows:

> **Dear Maui News,**
>
> *"In my last letter to the Maui News published on December 7, 1981, I suggested that the solution to the child abuse problem was embodied in the word Christ-mas, which literally translates to mean love-more. The news-media-oriented world seems completely unaware of the fact that everything happening in the world today was predicted to happen approximately 2000 years ago.*
>
> *Prominent in the news are world hunger, famines,*

earthquakes, violence, immorality, wars and rumors of other potential wars. Just recently, the news concerns a 'peace academy,' the 'Jupiter effect,' and the 'Shroud of Turin...' *The big news in March, and particularly on the 14th, was the meaning and significance of what scientists have called 'The Jupiter Effect,' a very rare astronomical occurrence when all the planets are grouped on one side of the sun....*

In 1981, the big news for astronomers was the extremely rare triple conjunction of the planets Saturn and Jupiter... In the Book of Luke, Jesus said, "great signs shall there be from heaven" ...In Genesis 1:14, God said, "...let them be for signs..." Is it merely an amazing coincidence that when Jesus was born, in 7 B.C.E., there was also a rare triple conjunction of Saturn and Jupiter just like in 1981, the year I rode the White Horse?"

In this long letter, I explain to the Maui News the signs of Jesus' second coming. I knew they would not print this one because it was a rambling manifesto about what the 'signs' meant. I ended the letter by saying: 'As southern Lebanon braces for a possible attack from Israel, the English armada steams toward the Falkland Islands, Central America boils over, Ireland buries its dead, the Afghans theirs, the Iranians and Iraqis theirs, we must remember that it is Love and understanding that conquers all. It is compassion and brotherhood that wins all battles. It is giving, caring and kindness that triumph over all. It is reverence and humility toward the one God of this planet that wins the ultimate victory.

Peace on earth and goodwill towards all men, for Christ is love and love is king."

On June 28, 1982, I wrote a letter to my friend Aaron Gold, columnist for the *Chicago Tribune*:

Aloha Aaron,

I was pleasantly surprised hearing from you. Unfortunately my mission on this planet is being ignored by the ones who can help the most, i.e. the news media. What you must understand and rejoice in is the fact that God has an immutable timetable for His plan on this earth and that He has me here to fulfill it. I, too, am subject to this timetable and, believe me, the monumental rejection I have encountered over the years has only made me stronger and more determined than ever.

If you recall, back in 1977, I spoke of credibility. I hoped that by now I would have bridged that gap with you and the Chicago Tribune *but, alas, history does repeat itself. 2000 years ago they said no messiah could come out of Nazareth in Galilee because Nazareth, much like Chicago, had some pretty rough characters and a reputation to boot; also, it has been prophesied that 'a prophet has no honor in his own land,' and Chicago has been true to form in its rejection of me.*

I have said to you in the past that I would never put you in a situation where you would be embarrassed. Unlike Thomas, who denied me thrice (that was part of the script and unalterable), God has given you, as He has given me, an opportunity to be instrumental in changing the course of history. In your letter to me, you said, "I really have no idea if you are, or aren't, but we need him now, desperately. The world is in shambles, no one cares or gives love to another freely..." I assure you Aaron, and we are both Jews, that our association is far more than merely casual or frivolous. *I have reincarnated to this earth plane as promised to save this world and not to judge it...."*

Writing this letter was a major turning point in my attitude. I was bold and not afraid to voice my beliefs about myself, which set the stage for my demise twenty-five years later. On April 15, 1983, I wrote the first of two letters to the Department of the Treasury, Internal Revenue Service, where I openly declared myself and predicted my future. It is important to consider that I truly believe, as demonstrated by the evidence of the past ten years, that I am the reincarnation of Jesus and a servant to God's will. Based on that, I am committed to whatever it takes to do the will of God.

Because the letters to the IRS directly contributed to my going to prison, they are not included in this book for obvious reasons.

There was no turning back for me; I became my studies. My personality by this time had completely integrated itself with the personality of Jesus, as portrayed by Dr. Schonfield, and I assumed the role completely, willingly, doing so publicly and openly. In my mind, the Federal Reserve was violating the Constitution of the united States of America, pursuant to *Article 1 Section 2 Clause 3*, which says there cannot be a direct tax on labor unless it is apportioned exactly the way the Representatives are elected to Congress. The 16th Amendment to the Constitution only pertains to indirect taxes and did not repeal *Article 1 Section 2 Clause 3*.

True to my words in 1983, "I am fully aware and responsible for my actions," the IRS handed down a seven-count indictment for obstructing and impeding the nation's tax laws and filing a false tax return. Facing up to twenty-one years in prison, I plead guilty in April 2008, to two counts. In December 2008, I was sentenced to 24 months in prison. On the day Barak Obama was inaugurated as President of the United States, January 20, 2009, 28 years after Birkat Hachama in 1981 I self-surrendered to the *Federal Detention*

Center on the island of Oahu. It was one of the most mystical days of my life and a day of numerological perfection. The only thing I was guilty of was putting my family at risk and turning their worlds upside down.

Everything was in perfect order. For the entire eighteen months I was in federal prison I kept a daily journal on an almost hourly basis. I was released from the halfway house on October 15, 2010. Spiritual history and the patterning of my soul had repeated itself. Jesus, too, had been indicted, falsely accused, convicted and punished as a criminal.

In the book, *The Jesus Papers*, by Michael Baigent, one of the authors of *Holy Blood Holy Grail,* it is revealed that papers written by Jesus exist, depicting his defending himself pro se (without an attorney representing him) in front of the Jewish council of the Sanhedrin, before the crucifixion drama. Baigent says: "Then my contact brought up the subject of the 'Jesus Papers.' At this, his wife became almost hysterical, waving her hands in the air and yelling loudly and angrily as she stormed out of the room. I could not speak her language, so I did not know what she was saying, but it was very clear she did not want those papers to be discussed."

As Baigent tells his story, the man who was in possession of these 'Jesus Papers' had purchased a house in the old city of Jerusalem and while excavating down into the bedrock in the cellar, in 1961, workers found remnants of an old temple, dating back to very early Christianity, and then discovered two papyrus letters in Aramaic, dating back to 34 A.D., written by a person who called himself bani meshida, which translates to mean the Messiah of the Children of Israel. He (Jesus) had been charged with and accused of calling himself 'son of God.' Jesus, in the letters, explains that the 'spirit of God' was in him and not that he was physically the son of God, but that he was spiritually an adopted son of God, explaining that everyone who felt similarly 'filled with the spirit' was also a 'son of God.'

Jesus is explaining to the 'court' that he is no more divine than anyone else. This author feels the same. We are all divine and that is why Jesus quoted *Psalm 82:6,* "Ye are Gods." *The Jesus Papers* is a fascinating book and definitely worth reading. When the Pope got wind of the existence of the 'Jesus papers' he asked Israeli experts to find and destroy them. It is obvious why. If Jesus isn't God, or at the least the Son of God, the church has perpetrated a huge fraud upon the world, going back 1700 years.

If these papers do, in fact, exist, then it will further strengthen the evidence of the past to present life patterning. I have represented myself many times in the courts pro se, even having won a case at the Hawaii Intermediate Court of Appeals level (the case set precedent). While in prison, in early 2010, I filed two section 2255 Habeas Corpus certificates of appealability motions to the 9th Circuit Court of Appeals, pro se. I was denied. Is it another amazing coincidence that both Jesus and myself represented ourselves pro se before a court?

While I was in prison, the Department of Commerce and Consumer Affairs of the State of Hawaii (DCCA) filed a Motion for Summary Judgment to revoke my real estate broker's license. After my release, on October 15, 2010, I reactivated my license with no objection from the real estate commission only to have it illegally revoked on April 29, 2011 in complete violation of *HRS (Hawaii Revised Statutes) 831-3.1 (a-d)*. "A person shall not be disqualified from...employment by the State or any of its...agencies...or be disqualified to practice, or engage in any occupation... vocation, profession for which a license... is required by the State... solely by reason of a prior conviction of a crime..." This will be addressed in my book about the corruption of justice in the State of Hawaii.

In August 2011 I asked Governor Abercrombie to help me get my license back. I asked him once face to face. Once with his Maui administrative assistant. I also filed papers for a pardon. The Governor deferred to the state agencies and did not take charge as Executive in Chief. My appeal hearing at the lower court level was set for November 2011. I was denied. Through my attorney I filed a motion for reconsideration and on January 5th, 2012, I was denied again. Governor Abercrombie declined to get involved, but it's not over yet. On July 23, 2012 I appealed to the Hawaii Intermediate Court of Appeals. On September 10, 2012 a three-judge merit panel was assigned to my case. On July 25, 2014 oral testimony was waived and my case went on the calendar. On December 17, 2014 my appeal to the Intermediate Court of Appeals was denied. I immediately began researching how to file a Writ of Mandamus to the Hawaii State Supreme Court, which I filed on March 23, 2015 pro se. It was denied on May 23, 2015 for no legal reasons. The real reason is quite transparent. The Hearing's Officer for the State agency that recommended the revocation of my real estate broker's license of 42 years is the Chief Justice for the Intermediate Court of Appeals.

"Then led they Jesus from Caiaphas unto the hall of judgment: and it was early; and they themselves went not into the judgment hall; lest they should be defiled; but that they might eat the Passover. (Governor Pontius) Pilate then went out unto them and said, 'What accusation bring ye against this man?' They answered and said unto him, 'if he were not a malefactor (criminal), we would not have delivered him up unto thee.' Then said Pilate unto them, 'Take ye him, and judge him according to your law.' The Jews therefore said unto him, 'It is not lawful for us to put any man to death.' Then Pilate entered into the judgment hall again, and called Jesus and said unto him, 'Art thou King of the Jews?' Jesus answered him, saying, 'did thou think this thing of thyself, or did others tell it thee of me?' Pilate answered, 'Am I a Jew? Thine own nation and the chief priests have delivered thee unto me: what hast thou done??' *John 18:28-31; 33-35*

After a lengthy conversation between the two of them, "...he (Pilate) went out again unto the Jews, and saith unto them, 'I FIND IN HIM NO FAULT AT ALL.'" Not only was I falsely accused by the Internal Revenue Service, like Jesus, I, too, was arraigned, indicted, convicted and punished for crimes I did not commit. Pilate could plainly see from his conversation with Jesus, that he was not a criminal and, for all intents and purposes, gave him a pardon. The Jews, however, forced Pilate into condemning Jesus to death by crucifixion. He really had no choice, but as you will see later it was Jesus who made sure he was sentenced to death, so he could fulfill the prophecies. Don't blame the Jews for Jesus' suffering and crucifixion. All they did was what Jesus wanted them to do. It was all part of God's Intelligent Design for humanity. It was all part of the scripted movie. It was just an act.

In 1984 Elise and I went to London again to claim the Ernest Digweed estate. We would do so again in 2002. I was told to hire an attorney. I left a copy of my newly published book, *My Past Life As Jesus-An Autobiography of Two Lifetimes,* with the office of the Public Trustee, knowing that it was only a matter of time before I made my reappearance on the world's stage.

Part Two

11: It is all based on cause and effect

There is still, a wide division between science and spirituality when it comes to the workings of the brain and the mind, i.e. that which is material and that which is consciousness and immaterial. Science is important to spirituality because of the critical verification process in establishing universal laws but science still considers mind and consciousness from a purely mechanistic standpoint. Scientists believe that consciousness and mind stem from the chemical and neuronal processes in the brain and are purely material states.

I Am Back-How A Soul Reincarnates attempts to bring science and spirituality into reconciliation by explaining the mystical process of reincarnation from the scientific perspective. Consciousness existed before any material forms came into existence. The material universe is around sixteen and a half billion years old with hundreds of millions of galaxies that are much older than our fairly new Milky Way. Our solar system has its own unique intelligent design that has been master planned by the Creator.

All that exists in the entire universe and the invisible dimensions that comprise the dark and extra dark matter are not even included in the count. Our concern is with human, our solar system and the unified field that makes up our system. The human body is basically a container that houses the replica counterpart known as soul. While a human being is in third dimensional space it is in a state of constant change. However, the intrinsic nature of our higher self, which is made up of soul, remains constant, eternal and changeless. The soul increases its vibratory frequency only during material sojourns or it decreases its frequency. Earth is our place to get the job done here and now to re-member and re-create who we are through our thoughts, words and deeds. It is through the thought process, independent of the brain, that alters the neurons in the brain and not the other way around. The neuro-scientists have it backwards.

Through the **science of pattern recognition** *I Am Back* establishes scientifically the existence of soul, the energetic vehicle of mind, memory and consciousness that persists even after death of the material flesh body. The brain is merely the material home to the mental states of consciousness. As said before, the brain is the hardware and the consciousness is the software.

When our soul re-entered earth-life it was in possession of every moment, every memory that preceded it, affected emotionally by all its previous lifetimes through the cosmic process of cellular memory. As shown before, each time the soul departs from its physical incarnation it takes with it the baggage of all the memories and experiences from that embodiment and all the embodiments from all prior lifetimes. The soul remembers the fundamental sensations of what being in a heavy gravity bound hunk of matter is about.

After some well needed R & R on the "other side" in the heavenly realms, the dimension, place if you will, between physical incarnations, the soul spends an allotted period of time ["there"] depending on its vibratory frequency. It could be minutes, hours, days, weeks, months, years, decades, centuries or millennia in our limited concept of time. The soul, always knows when it is time to return to earth or to other suitable material planes of manifestation to satisfy its karmic indebtedness or unfulfilled desires et al.

Remember, one year of earth time is only one day on the other side. *Ezekiel 4:6,7.* Time "there" has a whole different meaning. Think of it this way and you can do the math if you want to break it down to hours and minutes. When a soul leaves our third dimension of time and space at death and it is gone for one year our time, it is only a day for the soul "there".

When it's time to return to earth the soul will choose its parents, when and where it will reincarnate, and what sex it will be to further its growth for the greatest chance of success. The flip side to this is if the prior incarnation was one of backsliding and evil deeds the soul will reincarnate into a less desirable situation but still one that will enable it to pay off its karmic debts. It is all based on cause and effect.

If being a suicide bomber was the person's last act, it will repay in like manner the number of other souls in their host bodies that were killed. It's just the way it works. The *ninth chapter* of *Genesis* confirms this. "By their live*s*." There will not be seventy-two virgins awaiting the martyr. Unless the suicide bomber wakes up and repents its evil deeds, that is, change its course of direction to the light and ask for forgiveness it will die many deaths at the hands of other suicide bombers in subsequent lifetime<u>s.</u> It is the soul's vibratory frequency that will make sure the bomber is blown up by another bomber to repay the debt. Get it? So we all need to get our acts together. There is no glory or martyrdom in killing another human being. The opposite is true. The body harboring the soul will experience unbelievable hell once it has left the flesh.

The cells are permeated with all the memories of its past lives and now stored in the subconscious mind. On the conscious level the cell memory sends signals that translate into personality, individuality, character, habits, talents and tendencies. The cells are responding to those past life memories, the **patterns** of incarnations past.

We are in a constant state of cause and effect; past actions that cause present reactions. Our physical bodies and our conscious/unconscious minds are continually reacting to input from both the present and past lifetimes. The soul/body/mind is constantly reacting to the messages being sent from the subconscious based entirely on its past life memories about its past bodily incarnation(s).

Our uniqueness is assured and no matter how many physical incarnations it takes to get the 'karma' right we never surrender our history, experiences, or our original identity that is our eternal birthright from the Creator, the Unity, the Oneness that is God. Only in the extreme rarest of situations is a soul so evil that it must be destroyed.

Earth is just another school for learning, (We already know everything there is to learn but we have forgotten and must now re-remember) and reincarnation is the best tool that God gave us to assist us in the learning and re-membering process. It is worth repeating. Earth is a correctional facility. We are being tested over and over again. It's not too late to get it right. The Creator is very gracious and very forgiving. Once the mind is open to these concepts the neurons will change and adapt to the new positive energy impulses it is receiving. Re-membering is reconstructing your being.

Recent scientific discoveries about neuroplasticity show that focused thought of something produces affects on the brain. The conscious process of reincarnation of the soul is based on focused acts of thought, powered by will, attention and intention, and it is our own concentrated mental projections that create our external reality. Not only in the present lifetime but the lifetime(s) to come. The mind has the extraordinary capability to bring about complete self-transformation affecting the outside external reality through inner change and experience in the lifetime currently being lived.

Validating a past lifetime is accomplished by verifying the past life experiences which are recorded as the 'reincarnational DNA' of the cellular memory which is then translated into planetary energies revealing the actions of the past life experiences caused by the past life personality. Everything that makes up a personality is called the 'self.' This 'self' is divided into the lower and higher self. The lower self can be said to be "of the world." The higher self may live in the world of matter but is not of the world of matter. Self-transformation brings about transcendence from the lower to the higher. The higher self lives in an enlightened state, aptly called enlightenment while in the third dimension.

Let's re-cap the process.

The causal actions of the person creating life experiences are remembered and recorded as cell memory. The information is stored and then transferred to the future life embryo that is a suitable match vibrationally, planetarily, genetically and karmically. Upon death of the physical body the memories that are stored in the cells create a vibrational imprint, which are then translated into the myriad of energetic planetary combinations that make up a human being.

The greater the attention to mindfulness in the lifetime being lived in the present now with a focus of one's thoughts and actions on being loving, kind and compassionate towards all sentient beings, the higher, i.e. the greater the level of conscious awareness in the life to come. Cause and effect.

It is a very mysterious yet simple process and somehow the universe knows exactly when the celestial bodies are an exact match vibrationally to the lifetime just lived, and then, amazingly, it matches the energies with the right parents who have the right DNA that enables the reincarnating soul to have the same facial and body architecture from the prior lifetime whether male or female. It is truly a most incredible intelligent design.

So, the hardware of the brain is such that it is not fixed at birth and the neurons are shaped and molded to adjust to the cosmic energy grid of the soul that now inhabits the new flesh body. It was the soul's attention and intention that landed the right energetic combinations. *The more intense the attention the more intense the intention.* It is always the soul's intention to get it right "next time" in the next life. However, once in the flesh body the game changes. The conscious mind in the brain forgets on a conscious level the original intention. Ideas, intuition and favorable circumstances create the attention needed to remember the original intention.

As the child develops, the right environment can promote positive neuronal growth to keep pace with the soul's intentions made prior to incarnation. Everything we became in the past is now intention to become in the present. Everything we are now, our personalities, our beliefs, our habits, our values, our talents, our very character and consciousness is encoded in that cellular memory and is brought to life by the connections the neurons make in the brain.

The analogy would be emptying out the contents of an old bank vault that has become functionally obsolete and putting all the original contents that were in the old vault into a brand new one. The old bank building was torn down and a new one is built in a much better location. The vault changed but the contents remained the same. The *Vedic* scriptures put it this way. "The body changes but the soul remains the same." Jesus explained this very same process to the disciples in *Matthew 11:9-15* and *17:10-13*.

The situations we find ourselves in are of our own doing, not only from present life circumstances but also from actions from prior lifetimes. For better or worse we get back what we put out. Always remember; what goes around comes around. It is all based on cause and effect.

12: Pattern Identity = Person Identity

According to the Dead Sea Scrolls, Jesus was born on Sunday March 1, 7 BCE, a master frequency day totaling eleven (11) in the numerological system; i.e. (3+1+7=11). This matches the name Jesus which is also an eleven (11) in the Pythagorean numerological system shown in *The Prologue*. Jesus exhibited two master frequency vibrations. He was a double # 11. Any numbers that double are considered master numbers.

At the time of Jesus' birth there was a rare triple conjunction of the planets Jupiter and Saturn in the astronomical zodiacal constellation of Pisces. This occurred during the reign of King Herod the great who was born in 73 B.C.E. and died in 4 B.C.E. According to *Matthew 2:1*, "wise men from the east came to Jerusalem" looking for the birth of the King of the Jews.

The 'wise men' were Magians or Magi from Persia (modern day Iran) who were astrologers familiar with the biblical texts of the Old Testament. When they said in verse 2 "we have seen His star..." it means that they knew of the triple conjunction that month, and with their knowledge of the prophetic scriptures of *Isaiah* and the other prophets they deduced the exact time of the Messiah's birth. It was not a star, comet or other type of celestial phenomena. That is a myth. Astrologers/ astronomers would, however, have been able to see the conjunction in the night sky as a super bright star if the conditions were right. The conjunction became known as '*The Star of Wonder.*' Jesus' birth date of December 25th is a fabrication by the Church of Rome.

The prophetic birth of Jesus is proof positive of the intelligent design of the universe. The astronomical odds and improbability of one man fulfilling all the prophecies exactly as predicted from a thousand years and more before his birth is also proof of intelligent design. No human being could have contrived such an event. Why hasn't science given this extra-ordinary occurrence any consideration? The answer is easy. Wrong category. Religion.

The occurrence of the pattern of the number ten (10) especially the number twenty-eight (28) (2 + 8 = 10) is further proof of the intelligent design.

The next sequence not only demonstrates and verifies intelligent design it verifies hu-man has a direct say and influence on the outcome of that design.

Eckhart Tolle in his book *A New Earth* says that "Christ (Jesus) can be seen as the archetypical human embodying both the pain and the possibility of transcendence." Jesus as the 'archetypical' prototype of the Oneness of the unity is the standard model of reality for the intelligent design. Jesus is the created and not the Creator. Christianity needs to drop the 'Jesus is God' label. He was a messenger and a teacher for humanity to demonstrate that life on earth is but a real life drama. I have said this before. God is the chairman and Jesus was his CEO. When Jesus quoted from *Psalm 82:6* he was trying to make the same point. We are all God. We are all co-creators with God. 'You (we) are Gods and all of you (us) are children of the most high."

The will of Jesus is inextricably intertwined with the will of the Creator and of humanity and he does exactly what is required of him. Jesus is just as human as any human, however, where he differs is that he is super normal. Every human's goal should be to become super normal. Not being in an enlightened state (super normal) is abnormal. Not living in the illusion of duality is normal. Being united with the unity of the Oneness as a constant state of reality is considered super normal. When living in a super normal state everything falls neatly into place all the time no matter what the circumstance may be. Everything becomes simply as it is.

The Jewish group *Messiah Truth* (Google it) said that "Jesus did not possess the requisite qualifications nor meet the performance objectives of the job (of Messiah) according to the requirements stated in the Hebrew Bible. And as the historical record testifies (they say) the position of Jewish Messiah has not yet been filled and remains vacant to this day...the position of the Jewish Messiah remains open." The Passover ritual of Elija's cup attests to this. Their position stems from pure spiritual and scriptural ignorance.

Intelligent design created a blueprint for the messiah Jesus. And as long as there is a blueprint, the 'standard model' can be replicated.

There exists a blueprint for the archetypical prototype and is revealed in this book. The blueprinted and formatted soul that inhabited the body of Jesus has a traceable fingerprint that is the cosmic DNA of the blueprint of the intelligent design of hu-man. A prominent psychologist (remember, psychology is considered **a science**) explained that "<u>everybody has an essence</u> or a **'personal energy pattern'** which is unique and individual as their fingerprints." This is exactly it.

The premise is that the author, me, the reincarnation of Jesus, is the host body to the exact same encoded soul that inhabited the body of Jesus. The essence of Jesus, i.e., his ***personal energy pattern*** has the exact same "fingerprints" as me. The "fingerprints" are an exact match to the original fingers. The cosmic reincarnational DNA of Jesus' soul is traceable to the source. The process of finding the source is exactly the same as a CSI <u>c</u>rime <u>s</u>cene <u>i</u>nvestigation searching for the telltale DNA evidence. If you find a fingerprint then you should be able to find the suspect. The same for the cosmic reincarnational DNA evidence.

According to nearly two billion Christians on the planet there is no doubt that Jesus was/is the Jewish messiah. The fulfillment of the prophecies bears this out. But how can we be so sure that I am the real Jesus, i.e. the reincarnated soul? There are many out there today who claim 'I'm Jesus.' Or, 'I am the Christ.' Or, 'I am Jesus Christ.' The fellow from Puerto Rico, who, interestingly enough, was also born in 1948 as was Eckhart Tolle, has been on the television magazine 20/20 and has been interviewed by the media several times. This person is convinced he is 'Jesus Christ.' He truly believes it. And he has followers into the thousands. And there is a man in Russia who has long hair and a beard, wears robes and makes the same claim. Jesus knew this would happen 2000 years ago and said so in *Matthew 24:23*. "Then, if anyone says to you, "Look, here is the Christ!" or 'There!' **do not believe it.**" Even in November 2011 there was a man who shot a gun at the White House, sent a video to Oprah Winfrey claiming to be 'Jesus Christ.'

How can we be so sure that I possess the "requisite qualifications" of messiah? How can we be sure that "this same Jesus" has come as stated in *Acts 1:11*? I have already shown that I embody the numerological sequencing of the number 10 (encoded in the prologue) and especially one of the two encoded "perfect" numbers; **28**. No other Jewish male on the planet that looks like Jesus (more so in my youth) embodies the encoded numbers. Anybody that is not Jewish cannot make the claim that they are Jesus reincarnated. Jesus was Jewish and the criteria for the "same Jesus" is that he be Jewish. I am Jewish by blood through and through back to King David descended from his second son Nathan.

Of the entire Jewish population alive on earth today subtract the women and children. From those remaining subtract the ones that are not Messianic Jews, i.e., those who don't believe Jesus was the messiah. Since messianic Jews are an extremely small minority of an already very small minority subtract from this group those not born in 1948 when Israel was reborn. From those remaining, subtract the ones that believe they are the reincarnation of Jesus. From those that are still standing, if any at all, subtract those who do not have, at the very least, some form of verifiable 'proof' that they are the reincarnation of Jesus.

If anybody is left with the aforementioned criteria they must be versed in Qabalah, adept at esoteric astrology and numerology, and embody the planetary composite makeup of a completed tiphareth (Qabala) entity with full messianic circuitry integrated to reveal an archetypical 'Adam Kadmon' (Zohar) prototype of the intelligent design.

Rabbi Harold Kushner was quoted as saying, "I am quite confident that the most important part of a human being is not his physical body but his **non-physical essence** which some people call **soul**, and others **personality**..."

Let's take a look at the Qabbalistic *Tree Of Life* and de-mystify it. In its uttermost simplicity the *"Tree"* represents a human being.

References are to be found in *Genesis 3:22-24*; *Proverbs 3:18; 11:30; 13:12; 15:4; Revelation 2:7; 22:2*.

The "Tree of Life" is made up of planetary energies, which is what a human being is made up of. Human as the Yetzer Sephiroth (archetypical prototype/Adam) has ten (10) basic components. Imagine the tree of life as a game board like *Parcheesi* or a similar game. Let's call our game *The Game of Life*. The object of the game is to get past the karmic obstacles of duality and illusion, of earthly desires, (attachments) and get to the goal or the final destination of the game, which lies at the center of the game board. The goal is called *Tipareth* or the God conscious center of the "Tree" which is **Love**. Any human who chooses to play the "game of life" can win. **The goal of the game is to become love itself.** Then you have re-created yourself as a child of God because now you have re-membered your (higher) self.

Illustrations and photographs about the Tree of Life are not included in this edition, but can be found in *My Past Life As Jesus- An Autobiography of Two Lifetimes (2001)*.

For advanced players the game gets more difficult and the object is to get to the messiah level of the Tipareth of God consciousness and become Christ-like or love-like. No need to give up your day job or your marriage or become a monk or a priest or give up sex. All you have to give up is the illusion of your material existence and not the material existence itself. Get out of duality and ego and get into unity and Oneness. It will take a lot of attention and intention to win the game in this incarnation. Like the game *Monopoly* you want to pass goal and collect the $200.00. You don't want to go to jail (earth) again and have to reincarnate....again!

We need to become a master of the game, which requires that we become a master of our self. All the moves on the game board are vibrational ones. Every move closer to the center your vibration changes and so do your planets. Every material and spiritual obstacle overcome changes the arrangement of the celestial spheres. Every good deed has its own planetary reward. If you become a *Mother Teresa, Dali Lama, Mahatma Gandhi* or achieve Christ or God consciousness, in this lifetime, you will most likely earn the **'soul of honor'** planetary aspect. These souls are 'advanced players'.

The 'tree of life' (hu-man being) has ten (10) basic energies which make up the human entity. Kether at the top of the tree, which is the root or the #1, and the malkuth, the representative of man and the material universe and the #10. *Genesis 1:1* has ten (10) words and twenty-eight (28) Hebrew letters -The Hebrew word *Sefirot* means cipher. Once we have achieved vibrationally the right combination of numbers and Hebrew letters, (22 in all) the letters representing the planetary combinations of God or cosmic consciousness, we can recreate creation. That is re-create ourselves in full cosmic consciousness. That is what Jesus did. He deliberately and willfully re-created himself and in full consciousness created his next incarnation voluntarily. Almost all souls reincarnate involuntarily. Jesus re-created himself as Bruce.

Both Jesus and Bruce have the Sefirot, the cipher, and we are giving it to humanity again. Every move in *The Game of Life* is one based on actions and deeds, which carry vibrations. These are not mental moves. These moves are based on action. Love is an action and not a mental construct. The greater the good deeds the higher the vibrations and vice versa. You just can't tell someone I love you. It must be a demonstrative action because "actions speak louder than words."

The "Tree" then, is a human being's horoscope chart of the zodiac or their Mazzaroth. God explained to *Job* what is being explained to us now. *Job 38:31-33*. "Can you bring forth Mazzaroth in its season?" Study these verses carefully as it is an encoded message. Look up each of the words and decode the message. "Do you know the ordinances of the heavens? Can you set their dominion over the earth?" What's changed? I am asking you the same things!

The *Mazzaroth* is our astrology chart, our road map decoding our encrypted soul pattern. It contains the memories of all our deeds, good and bad. The deeds are the actions and the actions create karma. Just like the television show *My Name is Earl*. Earl figured out what karma was and he made a list of all the people he did bad things to because he wanted to pay back the karmic indebtedness by doing a good deed. It's time to play *The Game of Life*. Those good deeds bear the fruit of 'good, good, good, good vibrations.'

When a person dies and crosses over to the other side the remembrance of those deeds are preserved in the re-incarnational

DNA of the cellular memory of the soul. As shown before, but worth repeating, those deeds are then translated into planetary, lunar and solar energies that are stored in safe keeping until the soul is ready to reincarnate into a new bank vault in the new neighborhood suitable vibrationally for the soul that has the encapsulated memory of all the lifetimes the soul has lived in material worlds. There are countless material worlds and the only way to get to them is vibrationally inter-dimensionally.

Once the soul has planted itself in the womb of the mother it has chosen, it readies itself for another earth life to get it right. When the baby is born on its particular day, hour and minute, in its particular longitude and latitude, the sun, moon and planets and the zodiac sign that is ascending or rising at the time of birth make up its road map, its chart, its horoscope. The energies of these celestial bodies at the exact moment of re-entry at birth are essentially a very similar mix of energies from the prior lifetime. The energies are the fingerprints, the cosmic DNA of the soul but they are only mere potentialities. It is up to the soul working with its new host flesh body to make the intentions happen.

The horoscope chart is an astral personality portrait of the lifetime just lived with other traits from many other lifetimes thrown in for good measure. Everything carries forward as talents, abilities and idiosyncrasies. The reality is the character and personality of the soul stays nearly the same lifetime to lifetime until it starts making changes. Progression or regression is the name of the game. The choice is ours. Which way do we want to go?

The metaphysical application is as follows.

The zodiacal horoscope is the transmitter of planetary energies and governs its operation. This operation occurs below the quantum level at the sub-quantum level. This is where the cosmic reincarnational DNA applies.

The quantum equation is: the inner space of the soul projects into the cosmic mind. The cosmic mind processes intelligent consciousness as thought forms. Through super luminal information transfer the inner space of the soul is transferred to the outer space of the waiting embryo. Nothing is lost in the transfer process. Everything is ready for reactivation into the third dimensional reality.

On the material side of the equation, the flesh body with its brain becomes home to **the identical pattern of the captured spiritual essence of the individualized personality of the life just lived**. The planetary energies translate the genomes of the metaphysical DNA into a literal printout, which becomes the soul's sign and number. *Genesis 1:14* Then God said, "Let there be lights in the firmament of the heavens to divide the day from the night; and let them be for signs and seasons, and for days and years." Your 'sign' is your tree of life. The combination of all the celestial energies that is your 'sign' reveals the pattern of your soul. "Signs" also refers to cosmic events like blood moons, solar eclipses, major planetary conjunctions, shemitah years, et al.

In our milky way Galaxy there are many constellations and the most notable are the twelve of our Zodiac. Most fixed stars have an encoded meaning and every one of the celestial bodies emits a particular energy and vibration. The *Mazzaroth* astrological chart is an etheric generator that creates the software programming for the bodily human form, the hardware.

The constellations of the Zodiac, the corresponding twelve houses, the placement of the sun, moon, and planets tells the programming story of the soul. The rising sign determines the houses. If you go to an astrologer and have your chart done or you send in for a computerized chart make sure you tell the astrologer that you want a sidereal reading and not a tropical one. You are not who you think you are astrologically if you follow the tropical system.

The sign that the planet falls in describes how we express who and what we are. The houses determine the conditions and the parts of our lives where that expression occurs.

Each house emits a nearly identical vibration to its corresponding sign; e.g. the first house corresponds to the first sign of Aries; the second house to the second sign of Taurus, etc. So, a person could have, say, Jupiter in Libra, the 7th sign in the present lifetime and have had Jupiter in the 7th house in the past lifetime. The meanings are somewhat different but the vibration of the combination remains nearly identical.

Each sign or house is further broken down into three ten degree sections called decants. Each sign contains thirty degrees. The decants are made up of the three signs of the particular element of the sign. For example. Let's say the sun is in Aries, which is a fire sign. Of the twelve astrological signs, three are fire, three are air, three are earth and three are water. Each of those three signs are either cardinal, fixed, or mutable. Aries is a cardinal fire sign. If the sun is 15 degrees of the sign of Aries it would be in the second decant which is ruled by the fixed fire sign Leo. If the sun was in the third decant it would be ruled by the mutable fire sign Sagittarius.

Actually, the correct word is disposited and not ruled, but you get the picture. So, even if you are an Aries, and the sun is in the second decant you are an Aries with Leo characteristics. Astrologers don't emphasize this little nuance enough, if at all, but for past life purposes it is very important when reading the chart because a Leo/ Aries is ruled by the Sun whereas an Aries/ Aries is ruled by Mars and Pluto, which is a completely different energy combination.

It all depends how deeply you want to go in the exploration of your inner self. Astrology is a very exacting meta-science when it comes to a psychological profile but not quite as accurate on the predictive side of things. However, triple conjunctions of significant planets like Jupiter and Saturn are indicative that something is up and is important.

The combined placement of the celestial bodies of the sun, moon and the planets along with the nodes of the moon and their sign and house placement, how those planets, sun and moon are aspecting each other, i.e. how they relate to each other in proximity to each other by degrees, creates the matrix of energy that is reprogrammed back into the soul at birth. Even the strength or weakness of the aspect is a tell tale sign of the person's past life history. Like anything, it takes some practice to figure it all out, and like medicine and law you are always practicing.

The celestial etheric generator of the Zodiac churns out the software cosmic programming of each soul like a huge conveyor belt that goes around and around and never stops. When the time of birth arrives for the inbound soul the software is inserted into the hardware and we have a merger. The body and the brain are just the hardware and are inoperable without the cosmic software that makes it run. Scientists think it is the other way around, but as said before, that is not so. The ancient Vedic scriptures call the conveyor belt the wheel of death and rebirth that goes round and round for ever until the soul wakes up and 'gets it' (that is the Game of Life) and gets off the wheel. The purpose of this book is to help humanity get off the wheel and get free of death and rebirth. I 'got it' and I want to show everyone how to 'get it.' Remember: 'Master it or it will master you.'

Let's do a quick re-cap before we move on to Chapter thirteen.

1. The person dies; that is, the hardware became functionally obsolete and can no longer process the software.

2. The soul, i.e. the software and all the programming when the hard-drive (flesh body) crashed (died) was backed up and saved on a memory card with all the memories and deeds of the lifetime just lived. What a good analogy.

3. The memory card has stored the cosmic DNA of the encapsulated cellular essence of the soul and its personality, character, and individuality traits from the old hard-drive. The old hard-drive is defunct (dead) but the information (software/soul) lives on in the memory card waiting to be down/up loaded into the new hard-drive (flesh body). The process is identical.

4. The essence of the soul is stored now in spiritual space which is really the 'other side' where the soul goes between lifetimes to freshen up a little, go to the school of higher heavenly learning,

view and review the life just lived and if necessary view and review other past lives.

5. The soul prepares for its next lifetime on earth or another material planet best suited for the soul's growth, and then reincarnates when the celestial orbs are in the exact place that matches the energetic impulses of the soul's past lifetime. Most souls reincarnate within seconds, minutes or hours of earth time while the planetary energies are still energetically similar when the soul left the earth. The time 'there' for the soul is much longer because of the space-time disparity, i.e. 'one year for one day.' The combined celestial energies must match the soul's karma.

6. The soul and the memory card, through the process of super luminal information transfer, with the help of the genomes, neurotransmitters and neuropeptides, jump into the new hardware (the waiting embryo) sometime prior to birth. The time spent in the womb depends entirely on the soul's karma and the cosmic timing. More advanced souls spend less time in the oven.

7. The baby is born again (reincarnates) at the exact moment in time that the external planetary energies of outer space match the past life energies of the soul's inner space.

8. Now that the software has been programmed into the hardware the system gets booted up and the soul picks up right where it left off when it was downloaded onto the memory card.

9. That's how it works.

10. There are no guarantees that the system won't crash and burn.

11. The energies are but potentialities.

12. The soul in its new host body must work together to reach the spiritual goal of transformation, enlightenment, transcendence and liberation. Spiritual symbiosis.

13: The Seal Of Approval

It seems most likely that the super luminal information transfer of energy from the soul into the embryo happens when the neuropeptides, with the help of the neurotransmitters, moves the genomes of the encapsulated reincarnational DNA levels of the cell's memory (cosmic mind and cosmic consciousness) into the neurons of the brain cells of the baby that is ready for rebirth.

Intelligent design has the timing worked out to the second and minute when there is an epigenetic and genetic match of the soul's karma to that of its material bodily counterpart. All past life information from the super conscious is stored in the subconscious and only the new life's events become part of the conscious. Upon birth the soul forgets its divinity. When it re-members from whence it came and recreates it-self in the image and likeness of love, then it reunites with the divine. This is to be accomplished while on earth.

Dr. Ian Stevenson, past head of the Department of Psychiatry at the *University of Virginia* has documented over three thousand cases of reincarnation mostly of young children who had vivid recollections of a past life. Dr. Brian L. Weiss, former head of the Department of Psychiatry at a hospital in south Miami has also documented hundreds of cases of patients who, through past life regressive therapy, a.k.a., hypnosis, recall past lives.

Until now no one has been able to prove scientifically a past life through the process of the reincarnation of the soul. Science will never (never say never) accept reincarnation unless proven by the scientific method, which this book satisfies on several different fronts and through several different scientific applications.

The soul reincarnates into the new body with the intentions that were made in the period between lifetimes based upon the karma of the soul. This can manifest as unfulfilled desires, unfulfilled dreams, unfulfilled accomplishments, uncompleted projects, unfulfilled love, goodbyes not said and debts both material and spiritual to be repaid. The reasons for a soul's return are as numerous as the stars in the heavens.

On April 2, 1948 at 8:38 A.M. in Chicago, Illinois, the energies of the solar system were such that they formed the Messianic encryption. The composite combinations of the celestial bodies of our solar system revealed the 'requisite qualifications to meet the performance objectives' for the job of Messiah as set forth by *Messiah Truth*, the unauthorized spokespersons for the de facto body politic of the nation of Israel; the official debunkers of Jesus as Messiah.

As described earlier each combination of a planet in a sign and house, aspecting other celestial bodies in their signs and houses tells a piece of the puzzle of the story of the soul's past life personality, character, individuality, et al. and their history. From a purely psychological point of view the past life perspective gives the missing link to the person's present personality. Without astrology, in this author's opinion, psychology is an incomplete science, just as astronomy is incomplete without its sister meta-science astrology, and physics is incomplete without an understanding of metaphysics.

The stronger the aspect of the planets the clearer the picture of the past life and the potentialities created by the intentions of the soul for success. In the advanced *Game of Life*, the closer we get to the goal, which is the center of the game board, the planetary combinations become rearranged to reflect the game's goal, which is God, Christ or Love consciousness. As soon as we are at the center we go through an initiation to make sure we are qualified to pass go and collect the two hundred dollars.

Once initiated we graduate and get our masters degree in spirituality. If we want to go through the sacrifice required to get an even more advanced degree in God/Christ/Love consciousness a double doctorate is required. Anyone can achieve a doctorate in Christ consciousness.

The job of planetary messiah, however, is reserved only for Jesus and no other. It isn't exclusionary or elitist, it is just the way it is. This does not denigrate in any way the divine sons of Krishna, Buddha and Muhammad or any of the great spiritual teachers alive on the planet today and those who have passed.

We are 'all sons and daughters of the most high' and we are all divine. Jesus was singled out for a reason only known to God to be the object of the prophecies and the chosen messiah for the Jewish people and the world. Christians, Jews and Muslims all worship the same God and they should not be divided according to the *Koran. Surah XLII 13.*

The Mazzaroth will indicate what direction the soul should be headed by virtue of the record of its past deeds and actions. The fruit of the seeds of the deeds. If the soul has sown good seeds there will be an exact record. Bad deeds? It's all recorded in the record.

Dr. Deepak Chopra in *The Third Jesus* says, "The primary principle of karma is that every action works like a seed in the form of results. Jesus taught that every action has a consequential reaction, either here or in heaven."

To put it another way the horoscope of today is a result of the karma of yesterday. Yesterday being the past life. There are many planetary combinations that lead to the game's end. Chopra says, "The law of karma was binding as Jesus taught it [that] every action led to a result with moral weight."

Karma is binding. However, through the law of grace, a soul that truly repents and atones for wrongdoing can change its direction, ask God for forgiveness and break the cycle of karma. The word 'atone' really means at-one, i.e. at one with oneself and with God united after making the spiritual change of direction. Grace is the favor and God knows when the soul is sincere.

David and Jesus were in God's favor. *2 Samuel 7:14-15.*

"I will be his father and he will be my son...my love will never be taken away from him." *John 6:27*

"On him, God the Father has placed his seal of approval." *John 5:20*

"For the Father loves the son..."

What exactly is this "seal"? It is the Messianic planetary composite makeup of David/Jesus/Bruce. The "seal" is bestowed upon the one who has the requisite qualifications to be the Jewish Messiah; however we are all God's children and in God's favor; when doing the will of God we all earn God's seal of approval.

We know from Jesus' birth date on March 1, 7 BCE that he was born when the sun was in the constellation sign of Pisces. We also know that Jupiter and Saturn were in the sign of Pisces and that gives us a lot to go on. After thirty-seven years I was able to decode the birth horoscope of Jesus and I did it while I was at the *Federal Detention Center* in Honolulu, Hawaii. The sun would have to have been ten to twelve degrees in the Scorpio decant of the sign of Pisces giving us a deeper insight into the personality makeup of Jesus.

I was also born when the sun was in the sign of Pisces in the Scorpio decant. Since the birth of Jesus, the sun by precession has moved twenty-eight (28) degrees clockwise in the sign of Pisces. Taking this into account when I was born on April 2, 1948 the sun was no longer in Aries but had retreated clockwise into the sign of Pisces. The sidereal system is based on the actual astronomical placement of the sun, moon and planets and the constellation they were in at the time of birth. Had I been born on April 2nd two thousand years ago I would have been an Aries.

The key words to persons born under the sign of Pisces are compassion and mysticism. According to Webster's definition of a mystic, it is "a person who claims insight into mysteries transcending ordinary human knowledge". The code words for Pisces are 'I believe.'

In highly evolved Pisceans mystical tendencies are well developed and people born under this sign that are advanced have deeply spiritual connections. Jesus and Bruce share these characteristics. The explanation of the sun in the Scorpio decant is in my book *The Horoscope of Jesus -The Spiritual Anatomy of a Messiah,* to be published soon.

It is not a coincidence that both of my grandfathers were Pisces. Harry, my father's father was born in Ukraine, Russia on April 16, 1896. My grandfather Benjamin on my mother's side was born in Warsaw, Poland on April 3, 1891. Isn't it interesting that Benjamin was born on April 3rd and I was born on April 2nd? To be truly Jewish, the mother must be Jewish by blood or by spiritual conversion.

According to world-renowned psychic Sylvia Brown and acclaimed spiritual author Elizabeth Clare Prophet, Jesus was a mystic and taught mystical matters. Elizabeth said, "One of the central concepts of my teaching is that Jesus was a mystic who taught reincarnation. The Nag Hammadi text discovered in 1945 dating from the second century or earlier preserve Jesus' recent teachings-among them reincarnation. Some scholars today are reaching the conclusion that Jesus may indeed have been a mystic who taught both reincarnation, and the path developing our relationship with the God within."

Did Jesus have a pattern that was so set in his cosmic and genetic makeup that in each incarnation he manifested the exact same facial and bodily characteristics as well as his inner attributes and abilities?

In *Fingerprints of the Gods* by researcher Graham Hancock, the author describes a man who lived in an extinct civilization in South America thousands of years before Jesus. If the following description of this person was given to you without any reference points with which to identify, who would you have said the person was? Here we go.

The description in the ancient records that have been preserved describe this ancient person as follows,

1. Lean
2. Bearded
3. White man
4. Past middle age
5. Wore sandals
6. Dressed in long flowing cloaks, (robes)

7. Pale complexion
8. A master of science and magic
9. Came at a time of chaos.
10. Came to set the world to rights.
11. Had an authoritative demeanor.
12. The man had great power.
13. He worked marvels.
14. He gave the people instructions in how they should live.
15. He spoke to the people with great love and
16. Kindness.
17. He admonished the people to be good and to do no damage or injury one to another.
18. He taught the people to love one another.
19. He taught the people to show charity to all.
20. He was a teacher.
21. He was a healer.
22. He made himself helpful to people in need.
23. He healed all that were sick.
24. He restored sight to the blind.
25. He was gentle.
26. He worked great miracles.
27. At one point the people rose up against him and threatened to stone him. (See *John 10:31*).
28. Medium height
29. Walked with a staff.
30. Called the people his sons and daughters.
31. He traversed the land.
32. He healed the sick by touch.
33. He had blue eyes.
34. He had long hair.
35. He abjured the use of force.

Sounds a lot like Jesus doesn't it? It wasn't. It was a man named Viracocha said to have lived in Peru after the great flood. All the physical and mental attributes of Viracocha are identical in every way to Jesus and Bruce. Nothing has changed. The chances are good that Jesus was Viracocha in a past lifetime before the incarnation as David. (There were also Egyptian incarnations and incarnations in Atlantis.) The personality of David was somewhat out of character to Jesus in his early years, but the evidence is strong that Jesus was also David in a prior lifetime. See *Revelation 22:16.*

In Chapter 14 we delve into the actual Messianic composite of a completed human entity that has the 'Seal of Approval.'

14: The Messianic Composite

We saw in chapter 13 that Jesus was considered to be a teacher of mystic matters by many. If Jesus was a teacher of 'mystic matters' then he would have the same trait now carried over from the past life. If he completed the *Game of Life* and made it to the center of the game board (the tiphareth #6 seat of consciousness and the heart center) then he would have solved the mystery of creation, the meaning of life, and he would have earned the energy frequency given to such a teacher. Remember, in order to qualify for the 'requisite job position' of messiah the person must have all the attributes. All the pieces of the puzzle must fit together perfectly or the person so claiming to be messiah is disqualified.

There is only one astrological aspect that fits the job description. When I reincarnated the planet Neptune was in my 5th house, which means **'a teacher of mystic matters.'** This reference I found in the 1927 edition of a book entitled *The Message of the Stars* by Max and Augusta Heindel.

Okay, I got lucky on that one. Let's see if I am really an advanced player on the spiritual game board.

At the time of my birth the *Sun in Pisces* was trine, i.e. 120 degrees, to the planet Saturn in Cancer. The encryption for this piece of the cosmic puzzle means that the person is honored by being the **'soul of honor.'** The 'seal of approval' cannot be complete without this energy aspect. No one claiming to be the Jewish messiah can be without it because the planetary record is based on the past life (lives) lived.

Christ is an office, an energy, a vibration; Christ is not a person. Jesus should only be referred to as Jesus and not Christ because it separates him from the people. Christ does translate to mean messiah and in the universal meaning of the word, anyone can become messiah of themselves. The messiah, to the Jewish people, means something completely different. It is a particular person with God's 'Seal of Approval'. And that is what we are talking about. Christ literally means Love. 'Christ is love and Love is King.' Venus, the planet symbolizing Love when I was born was in the sign, Aries in the third decant ruled by Jupiter, the planet representing the sign Sagittarius. Venus in the 3rd decant signifies

mastership. Jesus was often referred to as **'Master'**. *Matthew 23:8, 10; 26:25. Mark 10:17. John 11:28; 13:13.* "Ye call me Master and Lord: and ye may well; for so I am."

Mastership can only be expressed through humility. *14.* "If I then, your Lord and Master, have washed your feet; ye also ought to wash one another's feet. *15* "For I have given you an example. That ye should do as I have done to you. *16.* "Verily, verily, I say unto you, The servant is not greater than his lord; neither he that is sent greater than he that sent him."

The code name for the sign of Aries is 'I AM.' At the time of my birth the planet Venus was just one minute shy out of 120 minutes at 27 degrees 59 minutes in exact conjunction with the fixed star Alcyone which is at 28 degrees in the Pleiades. Alcyone is known as the **foundation** stone. The number **28** is the encoded number and Alcyone is at **28** degrees. Why is this significant? There can be no doubt that Jesus was the embodiment of love. His message was of love. If he was that then wouldn't it make sense that he would be that same love now?

Combine the energies of the combination of Venus in Aries in the 3rd decant and its encryption is:

"I Am"

The Master

Of love.'

Jesus was the master of love,

Love is the **foundation** of all that is,

Jesus said to them, 'Most assuredly, I say to you, before Abraham was **I AM.** *(John 8:58)*.

Love is the foundation upon which all else can be built. Look at the combination. Venus/love is conjunct Alcyone / foundation. Does the Bible support this?

Ephesians 2:20: "...built on the **foundation** of the apostles and prophets, with Christ Jesus himself as **chief *cornerstone*.**"

Daniel 2:45: "This is the meaning of the vision of the ***rock*** cut out of the mountain, but not by human hands."

Isaiah 8:14: "...and he will be a sanctuary; but for both houses of Israel he will be a *stone* that causes men to stumble, and a ***rock*** that makes them fall."

Psalm 118:22: "The ***stone*** the builder's rejected has become the cap*stone*."

Matthew 21:42, Mark 12:10, Luke 20:17 "Jesus said to them, 'Have you never read in the scriptures 'The ***stone*** the builder's rejected has become the ***capstone.***"

I Peter 2:7, 8. "Now to you who believe, this ***stone*** is precious. But to those who do not believe, "the *stone* the builder's rejected has become the cap*stone* and a *stone* that causes men to stumble and a ***rock*** that makes them fall. '"

When the Great Pyramid of Giza was complete in its construction around twelve to fourteen thousand years ago the ascending passage was said to have aligned with the fixed star Alcyone in the Pleiades star network **28** degrees (see 'The Sphinx' reference at the end of this chapter.)

The Great Pyramid was built without a capstone in reference to *Psalm 118:22* and to which Jesus referred in the aforementioned verses.

The Great Pyramid symbolizes enlightenment. The Grand Gallery, which is **28** feet high (2+8=**10**) signifies liberty which numerologically equals 3+7=**10.**

In order to get to the King's Chamber, which is 19 feet, high (1+9=**10**) one must climb up (get initiated, enlightened and liberated) the grand gallery. In order to attain enlightenment we must do as God told *Job in 38:31-33* and "loosen the bonds of Orion, break free from the shackles of material bondage, illusion and duality and ascend to God consciousness, the ultimate source of liberation. It's all encoded, encrypted and just waiting for the release of its true hidden meaning.

The Great Pyramid symbolizes a completed human being who has gone through the initiation and has achieved his full human potential as One with the Divine … One.

The capstone, the rejected stone, means completion. Love is the completion. Jesus represented the completed perfectly human being. Perfectly human as in super normal.

It is very interesting that Eckhart Tolle in his book *A New Earth* says, "Jesus tells us to contemplate the flowers and learn from them how to live. According to legend, that smile of realization (enlightenment) of the Buddha (being complete) holding up the flower was handed down by **28** successive masters and much later became the origin of Zen." Why **28** successive masters? Because it is the encoded number. Is it just coincidence that there are **28** generations from King David to Jesus?

Viracocha was a **master** of science and **magic.** Assuming Jesus performed many of the recorded miracles, to the people, they would have appeared as magic. If Jesus was Viracocha in a previous lifetime and if I am the reincarnation of Jesus, then it only stands to reason that I, too, would be a **magician**. Would I not? All talents and abilities are carried forward lifetime to lifetime. Nothing is forgotten and nothing is lost.

The next piece of the puzzle of the 'seal of approval' is the energy frequency of the magician. When I reincarnated the planet Saturn was in conjunction to the planet Pluto that is the '**aspect of the magician**.' This energetic combination confers the ability to channel spiritual energy through structured systems like the media, books, radio, movies and television. This aspect also gives the ability to bring about global transformation. Now that would be pretty magical. All secret societies, ancient and modern, believe in the power of the magic of wisdom and understanding; the game board's center in the realm of God consciousness to which man can attain when he seeks enlightenment. The universe willing, the information in this book will help to bring about global transformation, which can only be brought about by each and every human being loving one another unconditionally.

Jesus, magician that he was, as an advanced soul, created his intention while in his flesh body where it is most powerful giving a greater possibility of fulfillment in the life to come. Creating his own future lifetime and re-membering every aspect of it, and then recreating it, is pure magic. If it is your intention to complete the process in this lifetime it is best that you get to work. This is how the soul reincarnates. It creates the future life by the thought, word and deed of it in the past present. Think carefully about this. The so-called "theory of everything" is bound up in this.

The Great Pyramid is a map in stone. The map of construction of a human being. The completed human being is a symbol of God's perfection and His intelligent design for humanity. The human being becoming soul being is the true representation of order from chaos.

Look again at the descriptive list of the attributes of Viracocha in chapter thirteen. He 'came in a time of chaos', Jesus, too, came in a time of great chaos. Doesn't it make sense that the reincarnation of Jesus would also be present during a time of chaos?

Look at the world today. It is a chaotic mess. Global warming, exponential glacial melt, overpopulation, rampant poverty, starvation, disease, hunger, rampant ignorance, rampant crime and gang violence; wars, civil wars, economic chaos, ocean and air pollution, out of control forest fires, floods, earthquakes and tornados of large magnitude, volcanic eruptions spewing huge amounts of toxic material into the atmosphere; religious sex scandals in the church, religious division, terrorism, suicide bombers, drought, floods, government cover-ups regarding UFO's and extra-terrestrial visitations on this planet on a regular basis. Political corruption, selfishness, greed, avarice, over-crowding of prisons, inflation, disasters related to oil, judicial corruption, abuse of power, extreme disparity in the distribution of wealth, drug abuse, child and spousal abuse, unwarranted control of the media, censorship, the degradation of the United States Constitution, nuclear proliferation, screwed up weather patterns, geo-engineering, genetically modified organisms out of control, the poisoning of our earth by the chemical giants and forms of illegal taxation. Chaos abounds.

December 21, 2012 ended that 25,000+ year cycle. The odometer has rolled over to zero. Is a transformed humanity finally on the horizon bringing chaos to its knees?

Is there any hope for humankind? Can any of the chaos be stopped in time before humanity destroys itself? It is hu-man that is creating this chaos and if something is not done soon we all may be in much deeper trouble. Are we now at the 'tipping point' or have we already gone beyond it?

Is the world going to maintain its intractable stance to being deaf to the truth of what is happening before its very eyes? Is this the legacy we leave for our children and our children's children? The information in this book can lead the world to the water but it can't make it drink. Governments are too arrogant and self-seeking and are not representing the people the way they should because governments are not We The People.

There is just too much division and not enough unity. Too much corruption. We are a world divided and separate. There is possibly a window of opportunity to turn things around but there is precious little time. Noah tried to warn the people to change their ways but they refused to listen. Abraham's nephew Lot could not find one righteous person in all of *Sodom* and *Gomorrah* and because of their wickedness those cities were destroyed.

Humanity can learn a lesson from the *Book of Jonah* in the *Old Testament* in *Chapter 3: 1-10*. God told Jonah to tell the Ninevites that if that nation did not change (repent) from its evil ways (excessive materialism, hedonism, narcissism et al.) it would be destroyed in 'forty days' time.' Lo and behold, the King of the Ninevites believed Jonah, issued a decree, the nation changed its wicked ways and, holy smokes, God changed His mind and didn't destroy Nineveh. The identical situation on earth is at hand right now. As bad as it seems it is not too late for humanity to make the change. Why take a chance with the attitude that nothing is going to happen to the planet? Maybe nothing will! But just like September 11, 2001 with the destruction of the Twin Towers an unsuspecting public at large would never have thought that could have happened on September 10th. The general public did not know the tsunami was coming in Indonesia and Japan the day before they hit or the earthquakes in Haiti or Chile. Or the BP oil rig disaster. All sudden events with little to no warning. Like the movie *2012*. 'We have been warned.'

Does this author possess all the pieces of the puzzle that will give humanity reason to believe he is the reincarnation of Jesus ready to make his presence known? Is now the time? According to the Mayans, who inherited the information from the Olmec civilization who inherited it from the Egyptians who inherited it from the Sumerians, who learned the information from the alien Annunaki, the cycle of the Fifth Sun came to an end on December 21, 2012. There were 1,872,000 days or 5,125.37 years in that cycle and on that date the days ran out. Thus, **'the end of days.'** '**The End Times**.' This period was known as the 'long count' for obvious reasons but in the scheme of things it wasn't all that long. There is a much bigger cycle that ended on that date.

Any astro-physicist worth his stars will confirm that there is a black hole at the center of our Milky Way Galaxy and that on 12/21/2012, our Sun and our solar system aligned, i.e. was in conjunction with the plane of the Milky Way Galaxy for the first time in 26,000 years. Since one 'Great Year' is 25,920 years long, which is the amount of time it takes our sun to make the complete journey around the twelve signs of the zodiac, going in a clockwise motion (the precession of the equinox) it only stands to reason that 25,920 years ago, pursuant to 12/21/12, the precessional sun entered the sign of Aquarius as it did on January 26, 2008. Each 'age' or sign, being 2,160 years long.

Scientists, astro-physicists and physicists can't say for sure what the implications are but it's thought that the gravitational pull from the black hole and the alignment of the Sun could have been strong enough to throw our earth system out of whack and off its axis and tilt. If that happened the shift would have affected the crust of the earth, which would have had dire consequences.

In the movie *2012* we get the Hollywood version of a possible real life scenario. The movement of all the land mass is called a 'crustal shift.' Researcher/author Graham Hancock discusses the topic in his book *The Fingerprints of the Gods* with substantial evidence that our earth experienced such a 'shift' in our not too distant past. The South Pole, for example, the continent of Antarctica was possibly 2000 miles to the north and had a temperate climate with ice only in its interior regions. It is believed by some very well educated scholars who have done tremendous research on the subject that Antarctica might be the lost continent of Atlantis which drifted two thousand miles south after the last crustal shift and froze over. The documentation is very compelling.

The galactic center event on December 21, 2012 was at twenty-seven (27) degrees one minute of the sign of Scorpio (sidereal) which is ruled by Pluto indicating fundamental transformation. Coincidence? Pluto represents fundamental upheavals and permanent change. The pull of the alignment could have created humongous solar flares with enormous amounts of radiation and solar particles bombarding our planet and heating up its core. This solar activity could have triggered a reversal of earth's magnetic fields knocking out all electricity, electrical devices and the satellite networks in space, which means a loss of most of our communication capabilities. We got a break. This time!!

The gravitational pull could also set off more volcanoes, earthquakes, monster hurricanes, tsunamis of gigantic heights and other supernatural aberrations of nature. Ancient civilizations knew all this and they knew the date of 12/21/12 thousands of years ago. Shouldn't we be sitting up and taking notice?

I believe if humanity can raise its consciousness level substantially, the aforementioned catastrophe scenario can possibly be averted by the reversal of the energies emanating from our planet that are intensely negative and dark allowing very little spiritual light in.

Maybe God will change His/Her mind if we change. (It isn't actually God that changes His/Her mind. We do the changing and the universe responds accordingly.) It isn't that we haven't been warned. We have, but not too many people take global catastrophe seriously, enough people thinking these Bible tales and stories are just myths. In many ways they are but they are mystical myths we should learn from and not repeat.

The global consciousness shift will create an energy shift, which should mitigate a great deal of the possible destruction if that indeed is the possible scenario. The thing that is different about 12/21/12 from the time of Noah and Abraham is that this date was predicted (prophecy) thousands of years ago back to the time of the Sumerians. The bottom line is the greater the preponderance of higher consciousness on the planet the greater our chances to minimize the effects of the alignment which lasts for years. 12/21/2012 was just the beginning. Achieving higher consciousness must be a united global effort. History does tend to repeat itself and it was Santayana who said, "those who do not know history are doomed to repeat it." Anything is possible. Better spiritually safe than materially sorry.

Because the precessional Sun is in Aquarius a mental shift can occur. The energies are also ripe for an enlightened state of collective consciousness for humanity. Everyone will have an opportunity to get with the spiritual program. There is a positive side to every situation. The galactic center can also be viewed as the 'heart center' of the Unity, and being aligned with it we are about to experience a collective re-birth. So instead of an ending we have a new beginning. We are on the threshold of global transformation. Will we reconnect with it? Or will we reject it and become like the people in Noah's day? The choice is truly ours. Remember Jonah to the Ninevites.

We have a golden opportunity to wake up on a global scale. Will anybody listen? Can the information contained in this book lead the world out of chaos? Is the handwriting on the wall, or is it just a bad dream that will go away in the morning? Astronomers said there was a unique north-south alignment of the Milky Way Galaxy on

12/21/12. When you add in the alignment of our Sun with the plane of the Galaxy and the other galactic idio-synchronicity one cannot help but think that something is definitely going on. Why would I be programmed astrologically the way I am? What need for a 'seal of approval?'

When I was born the *Sun in Pisces* was trine (120 degrees) to the planet Pluto in the sign of Cancer within six minutes of orbit. This aspect is nearly perfect and the power of the aspect is absolute. The Sun is at 12 degrees 46 minutes of Pisces and Pluto is at 12 degrees 40 minutes of Cancer. If you look at an ephemeris (chart calculating celestial positions) for April 2, 1948 universal time the Sun is at 12 degrees 39 minutes & 14 seconds. Pluto is at 12 degrees 39 minutes and 8 seconds, an aspect of less than six seconds of orbit. In space distance this is unprecedented to be this exact on this particular day.

What does *Sun trine Pluto* mean in the overall intelligent design? What is the global import? As shown in an earlier chapter Alice A. Bailey published a book in 1948 called *The Reappearance of the Christ*. Bailey, a world-renowned meta-physician and spiritualist said: 'The Christ will reappear at a time of chaos and great difficulty.' Just like Viracocha and Jesus. All astrologers will agree that with the Sun trine Pluto there is an ability to **restore order from chaos**, especially with such a (near) perfect aspect. The person who has this aspect (earned from prior lifetimes) is **"qualified to gain a position of power and authority who will assert his will based on a spiritual motivation with tremendous power"**.

Between the aspects of *Saturn conjunct Pluto* and *Sun trine Pluto* we have two major ingredients for sweeping spiritual change on a global scale.

RESTORE ORDER FROM CHAOS

GLOBAL TRANSFORMATION

Notes:

The Sphinx in front of the Great Pyramid is the head of a woman and the body of a lion. The 'riddle' is easily solved. The woman represents the sign Virgo and the lion, the sign Leo. The precessional sun was passing clockwise from the age of Virgo into the age of Leo.

Count backwards, counter clockwise from Aquarius to Pisces to Aries to Taurus to Gemini to Cancer to Leo to Virgo. Each age being 2,160 years and you travel back over 14,000 years.

15: The Makings of a Messiah

We are all the Messiah.

The next piece of the cosmic puzzle has to do with the intention of Jesus for the future lifetime. The *Sun* was in my *11th House* at the time of my birth and the code words for this placement are **MISSION TO ACCOMPLISH**. Jesus was on a mission and the mission was not completely finished in the past lifetime and that is why he said," I will come again," to complete the "mission." This combination also means the 'brotherhood of man.' Jesus often spoke of the 'brotherhood of man.'

Not only was the Sun trine Pluto the *Sun* was also *trine Mars*. The code words for this aspect are **DESTINY TO FULFILL**. Anyone who knows the story of Jesus will tell you that Jesus had a 'destiny to fulfill.' His destiny was to fulfill the prophecies. If he had a destiny then, and if he promised to 'come again', it only makes sense that he still has the same energy pattern and that it is his destiny to finish what he started; to complete the teaching of *How A Soul Reincarnates,* the subtitle to this book.

How am I able to remember all this information from the past life? Well, for one thing, as a **"teacher of mystic matters"** I am '**able to tap a super conscious level of knowledge**'. On April 2, 1948 at 8:38 A.M. the planet Uranus was conjunct my ascendant or rising sign and this combination gives me the ability to '**tap a super conscious level of knowledge**'. This is no accident.

If you read the *Old Testament* book of *Genesis* you remember how Abraham pleaded with God to save Sodom and Gomorrah? Who is going to be the representative for humanity now? Who has the credentials for this position? Who has the 'requisite qualifications? Someone is going to possibly plead humanities case before the Judge and it won't be the Pope. And it won't be Donald Trump or Hillary Clinton. We are all the representatives for humanity. Love is the only credential needed to qualify. We are all inherently qualified to represent humanity. "We are the world!" "We the people of the world."

On April 2, 1948 at 8:38 am the planet Jupiter was in my 7th house. The code words for this placement are a **STRONG SENSE OF**

JUSTICE with the ability to **NEGOTIATE AND MEDIATE**. We know from the New Testament book of *II Timothy 2:5* that 'there is one God and one **MEDIATOR** between God and men, the man Christ Jesus.' Is this just a coincidence? If Jesus was a 'mediator' then he would be a 'mediator' now. Everything carries forward from past to present. We know that Jesus had a 'strong sense of justice.' What's changed?

Besides being a mystic and 'able to tap a super conscious level of knowledge' I also have a '*strong sensitivity to unseen forces*'. This piece of the puzzle is the *Moon in the 8th House*.

The planet Pluto was in my 3rd House at birth. A person who has this placement is '*responsible for exclusive and secret information pertaining to matters of great importance*'. Anyone who has any of the aforementioned placements has earned them. By now we should have a very good idea how the "Game of Life" works. If it's your life's mission and destiny to 'save the world' (empower it) and you do something about it, your birth chart will reflect those deeds. Cause and effect. Remember, creation stems from thought, words and deeds.

Saving (empowering) the world takes a lot of energy. God made sure I had enough to get the job done. It has been 42 years of nonstop work and the energizer bunny is still going and going and going. *Mars was sextile* (60 degrees) *Uranus* at birth, which has as its code words '*enormous energy*'.

I had backup. *Mars was conjunct Pluto* at birth and its code words are '*able to tap the energy of universal power*'. The word of God has awesome power. Desire for bringing about the 'brotherhood of man' carries with it enormous power.

In the 1933 book *The Sacred Symbols of Mu,* James Churchward said that "Jesus did not teach a new faith but rather the original religion of man. He said **one of the cardinal themes of Jesus was reincarnation.** The original religion of man was the brotherhood of man based entirely on love of thy neighbor and loving kindness to all of life."

The book *Edgar Cayce On The Dead Sea Scrolls* released in 1970 gives many readings about an acetic group of Jews that lived in a community called Qumran by the Dead Sea in ancient Israel. While in trance Cayce said, "The Essenes, including **Jesus studied astrology**." Another book entitled *Edgar Cayce On Reincarnation* states, "The Essenes did astrological forecasts as well as all those records pertaining to the coming of the Messiah."

In trance he states, "We have a number of the Essene works, referring to the movements of the heavenly bodies. For them the stars and their positions could affect men's lives and amongst their esoteric documents we have one describing the influence of the heavenly bodies on the physical and spiritual characteristics of those born in certain sections of the zodiac."

The holy scripture of the *Baghavad Gita* from India says, "the type of body we have now is an expression of our consciousness at the time of our last death." *Verse 15:9*. Not only do we carry over all our talents, et al from the past, we pick up the same facial and body characteristics from the life just lived. It is just the continuation of the script of the soul, body after body, lifetime after lifetime until we jump off the spinning wheel of birth, death and re-birth. If we learn all the lessons of love we can get off the wheel. It is as simple as that.

In chapter fourteen we touched on two aspects of the planet Saturn. *Sun trine Saturn*, which means the 'Soul of Honor', and *Saturn conjunct Pluto, which* means the 'magician, spiritual energy and global transformation.'

In her book *Astrology And Your Past Lives* Jeanne Avery says that "the sign, house placement and aspects to the planet Saturn are hints about lives you might have lived and that the incarnating entity chooses the time most astrologically advantageous for its mission on earth."

When Jesus reincarnated as me, Bruce, *Saturn was sextile* (60 degrees) to my ascendant (rising sign). The code words for this aspect are *"**effective in positions of leadership**."* Saturn is also *sextile* to *Neptune, which* means "**he will work to make a spiritual** *contribution to stem the tide of social Injustice and be useful as a guide and advisor to individuals in power.*" Another meaning of *Saturn conjunct Pluto* is "***he will make far reaching and long lasting effects on the environment, ' and his ideas and projects will have a transforming effect upon the world.*"

John 3:1,2. "There was a man of the Pharisees named Nicodemus, a ruler of the Jews… came to Jesus by night and said to him, "***Rabbi, we know that you are a teacher come from God.***" Jesus was a "***useful guide and advisor***" to Nicodemus who had a close relationship with Governor Pontius Pilate. Do you see how this trait carried over into the next lifetime?

It is our character and personality that defines who and what we are really all about.

16: It's All About Personality

The Third Jesus by Deepak Chopra recounts an interview with Albert Einstein who asked if he had been influenced by Christianity to which Einstein replied: "I am a Jew, but I am enthralled by the luminous figure of the Nazarene." The interviewer was surprised by what he said and then asked him if he believed Jesus actually existed to which Einstein replied, "Unquestionably. No one can read the gospels without feeling the actual presence of Jesus. His **PERSONALITY** pulsates in every word. No myth is filled with such life."

Likewise, Dr. Hugh Schonfield, author of *The Passover Plot* said, "*The Passover Plot* is the outcome of an endeavor which has extended over forty years to discover the man Jesus really was."

Albert Einstein said, '**His personality pulsates**...' What exactly is personality? If I am truly the reincarnation of Jesus, then the personality of Jesus should be identical to my personality. If we are merely transferring Jesus' record into a new body (the contents of the old bank vault) then nothing should have changed between the death of Jesus and my birth. This is why *Acts 1:11* is so important, '**This same Jesus**' This automatically disqualifies all contenders and pretenders.

Let's examine closely the Webster dictionary definitions of Personality and Character.

PER.SON.ALITY

1 The quality or fact of being a person;

2 The quality or fact of being a particular person; **personal identity, individuality;**

3 **Habitual patterns** and **qualities of behavior** of any individual as expressed by physical and mental activities and attitudes; distinctive individual qualities of a person considered collectively;

4 The sum of such qualities as impressing or likely to impress others;

    5   A person; especially a notable person; personage.

'Personal identity' is what we are talking about. *A New Earth* by Eckhart Tolle correctly defines exactly what 'identity' is from the cosmically conscious perspective. He says, "Identity is ultimately no more than thoughts held together precariously by the fact that they are all invested with a sense of self. This mental construct is what you normally refer to when you say "I." In the seeing of who you are not, (the "I") the reality of who you are emerges by itself." The I Am.

Both Jesus and myself are acutely aware of our identity, i.e. the permanent identity of the 'I AM.' It is the eternal identity of the unity of the oneness to which we are all connected and interconnected.

CHAR.AC.TER

    6   A DISTINCTIVE TRAIT, quality or attribute;

    7   Essential quality; nature; kind or sort;

    8   **An individual's PATTERN or behavior or personality**;

    9   moral constitution; moral strength; self-discipline, fortitude.

Sylvia Brown, in her book *Life On The Other Side*, says, "**Our personality is part of our essence,** part of who we are, and part of what allows us to recognize each other, both at home and from one lifetime on earth to another."

I am showing you that I Am who I say I Am and who I was.

J E S U S is now B R U C E

CAUSE and EFFECT

Let's go *Back To The Future* of my life. Let's look at my script in the same manner that Jesus looked at his script when reading the scriptures of the Old Testament. Jesus was reading about events that were going to happen to him in the future that were written one thousand or more years in the past/future of his present life. He knew he would make sure the events happened exactly at the time they were supposed to happen. By knowing the time lines of the prophecies he could even predict, almost to the day, 2000 years into the future when he would 'come again.' This clairvoyance came from knowledge. The more you know the greater your vision.

The following astrological combinations in my chart make up of the 'Seal of Approval,' part of the composite Messianic makeup of my future that is causally predetermined. The release of this book will compel future events into the present time frame. Like the crucifixion drama, the time has already been appointed. In 1974 when I first began studying my horoscope, I was like Jesus, reading about future events yet to come. In an earlier version everything was in the third person. That was very impersonal so I changed the book to first person.

Pluto in the third house: 'What I think and communicate will have serious consequences.'

Mars conjunct Pluto: 'There is a tremendous power (spiritual) and energy in my actions.'

Neptune trine descendant: 'I will demonstrate my spiritual concern for man and give my interpretation of what is needed to improve the quality of life for everyone.' Love one another. Doesn't this sound exactly like Jesus?

Sun opposition Neptune: 'I will direct my goals toward fulfilling some important social responsibility.'

Mars sextile Neptune: 'I will stir up dissent to provoke necessary changes.'

Inconjunct Venus to Jupiter: 'I will generously offer to serve the needs of others.' Look at the list for Viracocha. 'He made himself helpful to people in need.' What's changed?

Mars in the third house: 'I will intervene in the world of public duties.'

Mercury in the tenth house: 'Destiny will require a show of eloquence. I should always be in front of the public because I have the ability to communicate with it.'

Moon trine Venus: 'I am good at public relations and handling people.'

Pluto in the third house: 'I will turn the tide from a hopeless situation to a favorable one.'

Mars sextile Uranus: 'I will challenge old ideas and doctrines that have outlived their usefulness.'

Neptune trine descendant: 'I will help to arouse every individual to use his or her highest values to make the world a better place to live.'

Jupiter in the 7th house: 'I have the ability and good fortune to bring into harmony all enmities and oppositions because I have a strong sense of justice.'

Sun trine Saturn: 'I am just in my dealings with all men'.

Sun trine Pluto: I have healing abilities and there is a magical property in the way I can transform others merely by my presence.' This is a future event and has not happened yet in this lifetime.

I AM BACK-How A Soul Reincarnates hopefully will have a transforming effect upon the world. The question arises. How does anyone really know what Jesus was like as a person? How do we really know what his personality was like? If you hung out with him long enough could you form a fairly good profile of his character and personality traits? Could you also get to know and understand his habit patterns, the quality of his behavior, his mental activities and state of mind? After awhile would you become privy to his patterns of behavior and would you know what his attitude was like?

Dr. Schonfield hung out with Jesus for forty years (so to speak) and reconstructed Jesus' personality and character traits. His portrait of Jesus was so comprehensive it could be categorized as a forensic psychological evaluation. When reading his book *The Passover Plot* you get to know Jesus on a personal level and not some deified version of him as the 'son of God' or worse yet, God himself come down to earth. Please! We are all 'children of the most high.' If you put Jesus on a pedestal you put him out of reach. That is not what he intended. He washed the feet of his disciples, hung out with the undesirables and did everything in his power to show the people that he was just a regular guy who had a job to do. He was a servant to God as I am now. (Does God need servants?) Nothing has changed. We are all made up of God. We are all the I AM.

Laurie Beth Jones accompanied Jesus for twenty years (so to speak), and published her forensic evaluation of Jesus in her 1995 book entitled *Jesus CEO*.

The psychological evaluations by Dr. Schonfield and Laurie Beth Jones are an exact pattern match. What is truly amazing, in fact, almost unbelievable, is that both evaluations of Jesus are a word for word sentence for sentence and paragraph for paragraph match of the horoscopes of both Jesus and me. The personality portrait painted of Jesus by both Schonfield and Jones is nearly indiscernible from my personality portrait. Based on all the evidence presented in this book so far, this is not surprising. It is expected. It cannot be anything less than an exact match. How else then will we know for sure if Jesus is now me? Any element of doubt must be eliminated.

In *The Horoscope of Jesus-The Spiritual Anatomy of a Messiah*, we get to see the exact cause and effect relationship between Jesus and Bruce. The reader will get a true sense of how the cosmic process of reincarnation works in its uttermost simplicity, i.e. if Jesus was like that then he must be like that now. Beyond a shadow of a doubt I am the identical pattern of my past. The personalities of both Jesus and Bruce are one and the same. Jesus is the 'what goes around' and Bruce is the 'what comes around.' Always remember that the seeds we plant we will eventually harvest. If not in this lifetime, the lifetime to come.

Let's re-cap and put the *Game of Life* and the game board in its proper perspective. An advanced player going for broke goes for the gold, i.e. the Christ or Messiah degree. He passed 'Go', made it to the goal and earned all the pieces of the 'Seal of Approval' puzzle. If you made it to the game's end, i.e. the center of God consciousness, the tiphareth, you won. Now you can teach others what you have learned. The following is a summation of some of the attributes of Messiah that I manifest in my horoscope/ Mazzaroth. Third person.

He is compassionate with well-developed mystical tendencies and deep spiritual connections. He is a teacher of mystic matters and a soul of honor. He is the master of love. He is a magician who channels spiritual energy to bring about global transformation. He will restore order from chaos. He has tremendous power and authority but his will is based on a spiritual motivation. He has a mission to accomplish and a destiny to fulfill. He has a strong sense of justice, and an ability to mediate. He is able to tap a super conscious level of knowledge, has a strong sensitivity to unseen forces and is responsible for information of great importance. He is a natural leader with enormous energy able to tap the energy of universal power.

17: Creation, Jacob's Ladder, Hu-Man

"THERE IS AN ANCIENT UNDERSTANDING that God was mysteriously active for a period of time before the creation itself—and that of this activity we have been given certain glimpses. Have you ever wondered, 'But what was there before there was anything?'"

The Qabalists claim that God's 42-lettered name (4 + 2 = 6; remember, the perfect numbers are 6 and 28) alludes specifically to this pre-creation activity. So even if the world did not exist physically (before formless and void), there came into being, as it were, a thought in the mind of God.

What follows is an interpretation of what I believe was in the mind of God before material Creation. I will also explain pre-creation activity. 'The Qabalists say that, before creation, God filled all of eternity perfectly and uniformly.' In this period of non-time, God drew His/Her blueprints and created His/Her non-material archetypical prototypes. When these were finished approximately 14.5 to 16 billion years ago in linear time, They uttered 10 utterances and Zap! Bam! BIG BANG! and created the 10 dimensions of the material universe.

'And he (Jacob) dreamed and behold a ladder set up on the Earth, and the top of it reached to heaven; and behold the Angels of God ascending and descending on it.' *Genesis 28:12*

The Biblical six days of pre-creation was the non-time God took to create the 10 dimensions before they uttered them 10 times into material manifestation. The non-time of this pre-material creation could possibly be calculated into trillions of years in our perception of linear chronological Earth time. God's plan and blueprint for everything to be material was created first in the non-material realm. God's thought of all things preceded the material things themselves. The act of creation is a process. We think thoughts in the form of ideas, and we either act on those thoughts or let them pass by.

Imagine for a moment your thoughts without your flesh body attached. Take this idea to the highest level into the mind of God. God, too, had thoughts and created what They thought, just like we would do here on Earth. For example, we get an idea; we have a thought for an invention and decide to act upon the thought and set about to build in the material what was non-material in our thoughts. The thought already existed before we thought of it. God had already created that thought. We merely tuned into the vibratory frequency of that particular thought form to convert it from non material to material. Thought to thing. From no thing to some thing. Nothing to something.

The Adam and Eve story is the allegorical representation of the pre-creation process before the material manifestation of it—before the 10 physical dimensions came into material existence. The "Fall of Adam" represents the creation process of involution from the highest plane of God (Kether, the number 1, the Unity, Oneness, aleph, alpha) to the lowest planes of nonphysical matter before physical matter came into existence.

In this fall/descent, all the archetypes were created by God, including hu-man, represented by Adam Kadmon, who, according to the Qabalists, was the first archetypical prototype in the involutionary and evolutionary process of creation.

Adam, as is shown in *My Past Life As Jesus-An Autobiography of Two Lifetimes*, translates to mean Man/10 and is the crowning glory of God's creation. God first had the thought and then designed the archetypical thought form long before the material archetypical prototype of the flesh form ever came into manifestation.

We are not trying to answer the question of how God came into existence. Even if we knew or could find the answer, that would simply prompt a new question of how the creator of God came into existence, and the questioning would go on forever. It is enough to ponder and digest the premise in this book, that hu-man was created in the image of God. We, as humans, are the ultimate, created manifestation of intelligence in bodily form and are here to re-member and re-create ourselves as who we really are.

One of the objects of *I AM BACK* is to explain as simply as possible the pre-material state to better understand the physical/material state of being. Since religions have labeled the place of afterlife as heaven* above, the earth plane represents the below. As the saying goes, "As above, so below." * H E A V E N = 28; 2+8=10; 1+0=1

The physicist's dilemma is what was before the Big Bang, if anything? To understand what went before the Big Bang and the material universe, we must climb Jacob's ladder and stand on the top rung and peer out into this spiritual realm, or dimension.

The building blocks of pre material creation are the same in principle as those of the material creation. Matter and antimatter. Atomic and subatomic. Quantum and sub quantum.

Pre material Adam/Man, as cosmic atom, is manifested intelligence. This pre-material atom of Adam/Man is composed of:

ELECTRONS	The cosmic force to receive	**EVE**
PROTONS	The cosmic force to share	**ADAM**
NEUTRONS	The cosmic glue as binding influence or restriction of the electrons and protons.	

As all comes from 'above' (inner space) the electrons as the receptive force are the root of intelligence. Adam as the proton combines with Eve the electron. Adam shares his protons with Eve's electrons, who receive them.

The primordial force and interaction of the cosmic electrons, protons, and neutrons, once integrated, becomes the vehicle or chariot of the atom/Adam or manifested intelligence of God.

This is the basis of creation.

So, at the very top of the ladder of creation is:

I	GOD	I
I	THE	I
I	ABSOLUTE	I

I Top Rung of Jacob's Ladder I

To properly understand the Qabalistic *Tree of Life* of *Genesis* and *Revelation*, one must stand the tree on its head. The roots are God. Everything under the sun is rooted in God, rooted in Love. The leaves represent material manifestation in the material world. The trunk is the ladder of descent and ascent of the Angels of *Genesis 28:12*.

What does God represent as the root of all things? All religions equate God with Love. Love is an abstract concept with many definitions. To maintain a scientific, rather than philosophic construct is the object of this chapter. Love, for example, can only be defined in the human context, as an embodiment of the abstract concept.

God/love represents absolute consciousness and absolute knowledge. Consciousness and knowledge yield absolute intelligence, which are conveyed through thought forms.

```
              |
              |
   _____
  |                        |
  |    CONSCIOUSNESS       |
  |_____|
  |                        |
  |      KNOWLEDGE         |
  |_____|
  |                        |
  |     INTELLIGENCE       |
  |_____|
              |
              |
   _____
```

The next rung on the ladder of creation is energy, for without energy, consciousness, knowledge, and intelligence can do nothing, i.e. no thing. One of the objects of God is to create things. Without the force of energy, there can be no-thing. Everything would remain with God, not created, un-manifested, in His/Her mind only.

```
|           LIGHT            |
            |
            |
|          ENERGY            |
            |
            |
```

Consciousness, knowledge, and intelligence, integrated with energy, yields or gives rise to the entire creative/creation process.

The next rung on the ladder, then, is:

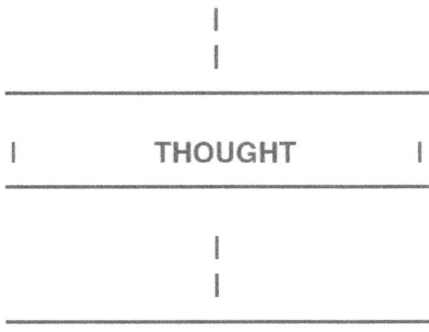

Thought is the byproduct of the combination of consciousness, knowledge and intelligence activated by the force of energy. The natural process of energetic thought is creation and is thus the next rung of the ladder.

The Involuntary Fall of Adam

where the top rung = LOVE

and the rest are mental planes

GOD THE ABSOLUTE
CONSCIOUSNESS
KNOWLEDGE
INTELLIGENCE
LIGHT
ENERGY
THOUGHT
CREATION
CAUSATION
EFFECTUATION

CREATION

Creation implies energetic, intelligent, conscious action and is a process. Creation is not solely an act of God. Hu-man does the acting and co/creating.

Energy as the active agent alone is neither constructive nor purposive. To construct with purpose the energy must have a guiding, directing intelligence that comes from the absolute knowledge and consciousness of God. Energy without God can do no-thing constructive.

The process of cosmogony or creation, made up of the activated ingredients of creative intelligence and energy, yields causation, the next rung on the ladder in our descent to matter.

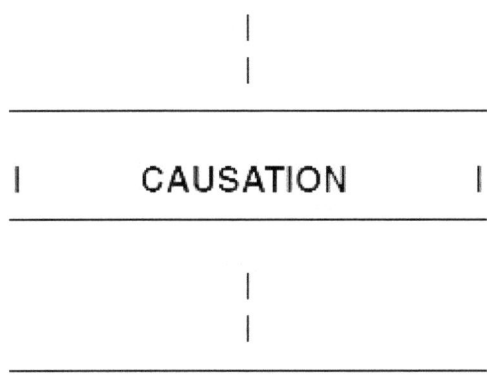

To better comprehend the nature of the parallel universe, the immaterial world of spirit and the material world of matter, we must enter into the mind of God to grasp why He/She bothered to create anything or everything.

There is a simple explanation. In his book *The Art of Loving*, Aldous Huxley says quite accurately that love is an action. If love is not actively demonstrated through actions, the love only exists as a mental concept. The action deems it a construct. Thus the saying, "Actions speak louder than words."

God, being Love, could only do the natural thing; to give and to share of Him/Herself. This is the process. When Hu-Man is fully activated in the flesh, the action of Love can manifest. To give and to share Love is the act of intelligent thought. It is the highest form of consciousness. The knowledge or the knowing of this principle and applying it while in the flesh body is the intelligent thing to do. The scientific application of this principle is explained in the words, "Love thy neighbor as thyself," because thyself and the neighbor are both God. This exists without conditions. Of the Ten Commandments, the first two are the most important of all.

Once the principal action of Love is fully activated in the physiognomy of the human being, the energetic field of the now-integrated circuits takes a quantum leap in consciousness. This leap is called Christ Consciousness, or God Consciousness. This Consciousness is a vibratory frequency and knowing and applying the principles of this Love / Christ / God Consciousness is what the mystics call the enlightened state, which is permanent and everlasting.

The *Book of Genesis* is the Qabalistic explanation of involutionary creation, which involves the life/love principle and its journey (the Fall) to matter. There is no such thing as original sin. Matter was the ultimate destination of God's manifested intelligence in Hu-Man and part of the Intelligent design. It is part of God's Great Master Plan.

Material flesh Adam didn't sin. This is a construct of the church, of religion, of (ignorant) priests and popes. The only sin is the ignorance of not knowing the process and the principles in the re-creation process. Not knowing who we truly are and not knowing the principles and the rules that govern the material realm, one cannot adhere to the process of re-creation and re-membering and, thus, one gets into trouble spiritually and materially and incurs karmic debts and we miss the mark. That is sin.

As we proceed down the ladder, we fall closer to the creation and the development of matter in the involutionary process where our symbolic Adam and Eve, representing the two principles of consciousness and energy, combine or become **united/28** to become matter.

Adam Kadmon, on the involutionary side of creation, represents the life principle of the *Tree of Life*. Eve, on the evolutionary side of creation, represents the Tree of Knowledge and the life principle in matter, or life's experience with matter, and thus subject to the laws of matter.

It is a logical progression in the 'fall' that causation will yield effects. Another rung. As the creative intelligence is energetically activated and descends, the radiation of the vibratory frequency in the process slows tremendously until the radiation begins to congeal, as water slowly does to become ice. Before water, came hydrogen and oxygen gas. The process is in principle the same; ice is the polar opposite of the invisible hydrogen gas. Matter and the material realm is the opposite of immaterial spiritual space.

All the rungs on the ladder thus far can be called mental matter.

HYDROGEN GAS	
OXYGEN	
(Steam)	
WATER	
ICE	

Steam is lightly congealed water of the hydrogen/oxygen. It is visible, transparent, and material. It isn't dense like water or ice. The analogy in the creation process is the same.

We are witnessing the fall of the building blocks of the life principle into its final destination, matter.

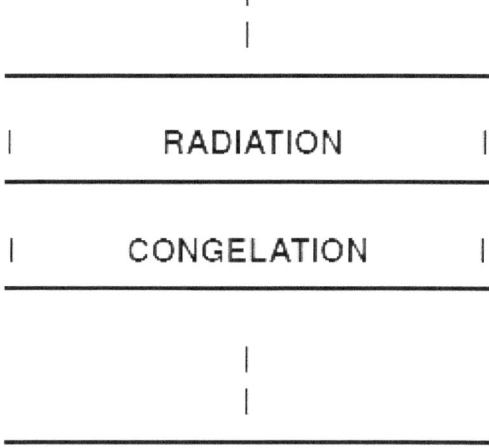

Radiation is the next rung on the ladder and, as the vibratory rate slows, the process of congelation takes place. All that is congealing, really, are the above ingredients propelled downward by the energy of the elements of the involutionary process.

The next rung on the ladder is the proverbial clay that can now be molded into all the archetypes that one day will **involve** into matter. This rung is congelation. The name of the congealed radiated energy vibrating at a now-low rate (but still incredibly high compared to the vibratory rate of physical matter) is called astral matter and is the next rung on the ladder. This level on the involutionary ladder is called the astral plane. These are the heavens. They are divided into levels, the top being the famous 'seventh heaven.' *
* "The natural world...a marvelously ingenious and **unified mathematical scheme**..." Physicist Paul Davies

HEAVEN=28
Eve UNITED=28 with Adam.
28 is the encoded and perfect number
4-2-1948=28. Bruce's birth date
430687=28. Bruce's birth certificate number
XXX-XX-XXXX = 28. Bruce's social security number

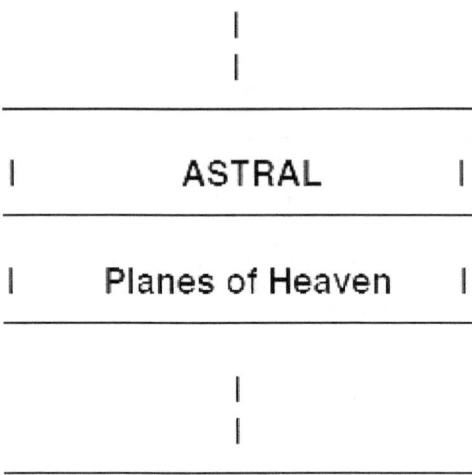

This is the place where we can apply the principles of nuclear physics at the subatomic and sub quantum levels of material reality. At the astral levels, we witness the result of the congelation through the process of fission and radiation of the cosmic electrons, protons, and neutrons of Adam's atoms yielding the life principle.

Atoms in the metaphysical context are forms of intelligence. In the descent toward physical matter, the motivating force of the atoms above becomes intense.

At the astral level, the Adam and Eve principle of positive and negative energies imbued with consciousness becomes even more intense. Like the swimming sperm to the egg, the positive proton energy of Adam wants to share its life principle with Eve, whose negative electron charge wants to receive it.

When God breathed life into the nostrils of Adam, it symbolized the cosmic creation process. The life principle that Adam represents in the involutionary fall to matter is still spiritual (or spirit matter in terms of the stuff or substance it is made out of). The soul is made up of this stuff. The soul is encased in an astral body, an etheric body, and, once arriving in the material world, in a flesh body.

As the spiritual conscious force vibrates even slower than the astral, it becomes ether-like, or etheric. Ghosts and apparitions are made up of this substance. Etheric matter becomes the next rung on the ladder.

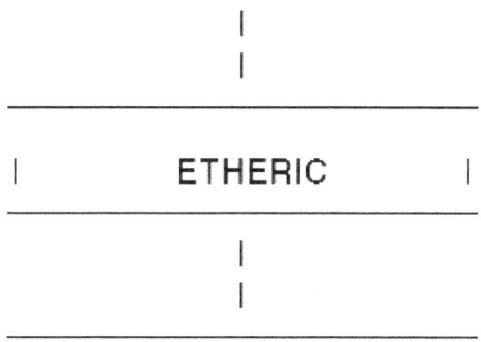

The Ether is like steam, but much more subtle and invisible.

As we fall ever so close to physical matter in the entire creative process, the cosmically conscious intelligent force of the spirit of God will ultimately surrender its conscious spiritual nature to the energetic cosmic gravitational pull to dense matter where eventually it will become clothed in flesh and forget temporarily from whence it came. This is the eating of the forbidden fruit of the tree of knowledge in the garden of Eden. Eden symbolizes earth. Being cast out of the garden of Eden is the symbolic leaving of the spiritual world for the material world. The creation process moves from the involutionary planes of spiritual anti-matter to the evolutionary planes of physical matter.

The last rung on the ladder is:

| DENSE PHYSICAL MATTER |

Dense physical matter vibrates at the slowest rate and is thus fully congealed, like Jell-O. A hot boiling substance has cooled to become congealed mass. The creative principle has now temporarily lost its spiritual nature by becoming immersed in matter. Heat the Jell-O up to steam and it becomes etheric again.

The whole process of creation, from the no-thing of involution to physical matter (some-thing) of evolution, gives us the whole picture. Physics and science have only given one half of the whole picture, the after or evolutionary sequence following the Big Bang. The word 'genesis' means birth, origin, a beginning, creation; the way in which something is formed; origination, formation, evolution. The word 'genetic' means 'of the genesis, or origin of something.

Genetics has to do with the material and evolutionary side of creation, but the 'birth,' 'origin', and 'beginning' came from something and not no-thing. A cosmic paradox. The some-thing are those involutionary planes of pre physical manifestation. As shown, the process at the highest mental planes displays no form and is inherently primordial. Primordial means first to begin; first in time; existing at or from the beginning; underived; fundamental original. In biology, earliest formed in the development of an organism. "And God said, I Am the beginning and the ending."

Now we have our final basis for understanding the complete picture. The Big Bang was not the beginning. Genesis is the sojourn of spirit in its fall to matter. Exodus is the journey through matter, the escape from the bondage in Egypt (**28**), which is matter, Malkuth (**10**). *I AM BACK* represents the pre-redemption and re-creation of matter back to the Father (Spirit). In the biological definition of 'primordial,' we glean a major clue.

- Earliest formed organism (in matter) is evolutionary and material.

- God, as the 'primordial underived,' is the true beginning. Everything came from nothing first, no-thing.

- God — earliest unformed, no-thing, no-form.

- Involutionary/Epigenesis.

'Epigenesis' means after, upon, plus genesis, birth, descent. In biology, it is the theory that the germ cell is structure less and that the embryo develops as a new creation through the action of the environment on the protoplasm. (*Webster's New World Dictionary* 1962 p. 603)

- The entire process of creation* from the underived absolute God to the fall to matter is epigenetic.

☐	Epigenetic	Involution
		Immaterial
☐	Genetic	Evolution
		Material

Let's look at the completed process of cosmic epigenesis in our 'ladder' illustration.

* Here is the creation process in more understandable human terms. Since God is Love everything from God is an act of Love. When cosmic Adam and cosmic Eve UNITED in LOVE they had a cosmic climax, a cosmic orgasm of LOVE and the stage was set for the birth (Big Bang! Ha!) of the material universe. L O V E = 9. Completion. The epigenetic process of creation was completed in that act of Love. Genesis 1:27=10. We humans are created in the image of God by an act of Love. We ARE love.

| GOD |
| THE |
| ABSOLUTE |

| Top Rung |
| CONSCIOUSNESS |
| KNOWLEDGE |
| INTELLIGENCE |
| **LIGHT** |
| ENERGY |
| THOUGHT |
| CREATION |
| CAUSATION |

	EFFECTUATION	
	RADIATION	
	CONGELATION	
	ASTRAL MATTER	
	ETHERIC MATTER	
	DENSE PHYSICAL MATTER	
	BOTTOM RUNG	
	EARTH	

By definition epigenesis states that 'after' and 'upon' precede genesis followed by birth and descent, because the process recognizes that something structure less already exists and then things develop, upon the impulse from God. The embryo is born. The embryo must precede the birth.

So the embryo of consciousness, knowledge, intelligence, energy and thought develop as a new creation though the action of the environment on the protoplasm.

	Earth - Eden	
	Egypt - Matter	
	Spirit Enslaved in Matter	

The embryo is going to develop into God's ultimate new creation, Adam /Man. This is as a result through the action of the environment on the protoplasm, embryo of man. Let's define the action of the environment. The environment, pre-embryonic, is still basically formless, but consists of:

CONSCIOUSNESS
KNOWLEDGE
INTELLIGENCE
LIGHT
ENERGY
THOUGHT
CREATION

This is the cosmic environment. Creative intelligence and energy bring about:

CAUSATION
EFFECTUATION
RADIATION

The new creation, through the process above, goes into the cosmic pressure cooker for the next step in the epigenetic process.

CONGELATION

The cosmic embryo of the pre material human embryo is now the congealed protoplasm of the astral and etheric planes of manifestation. God took a total of 6 (a perfect number) days for the epigenetic creation. One such day maybe equal to a trillion or quadrillion more of our linear years. The total 7 days (6 + 1) of the material genetic creation may have been somewhat shorter, say 4.5 to 14.5 billion years in linear time, because the planning, blueprints, and archetypes already were created in the immaterial dimensions in the epigenetic process.

What is truly amazing is that God delineated the entire framework mathematically in a format so we can understand, discover, comprehend, and re-member our true inherent nature, which is Godlike, which is hu-man like, since we are created in the Creator's image. God and Hu-Man are One. Now that we re-member and have re-created who we really are, we become soul beings.

When Jesus referred to himself as the Son of Man throughout the Gospels and not the Son of God, he was acknowledging these metaphysical epigenetic principles. There is no one 'son of God'.

There is no 'only begotten son'. 'There is however an archetypical prototype of God's children called Adam Kadmon in the Qabala and Zohar who eventually became known as the personality of Jesus (Emmanuel) which means 'God with us, ' because Jesus was completely and perfectly human, always living in the presence of God. Emmanuel doesn't mean 'God with me.'

This Son of Man would recreate and live out the prophecies to reenact the epigenetic fall of Adam. The earth life represents the sacrifice of the flesh for the spirit in the evolutionary ascent back to God. The involutionary descent is the sacrifice of the spirit for the flesh. 'What goes around, comes around.' The 'second coming' is the what comes around and is the next step in the evolutionary process and logically the next step for humanity.

The descent and ascent of Hu-man are both governed by gravity. As one's consciousness is raised, gravity decreases and one feels spiritually lighter. The closer one gets to the light of the wisdom of God, the closer one gets in the desire to share, to give, and to love. As the desire to receive this knowledge is the root of intelligence, the desire to share it is the light of wisdom. Applying this knowledge is God-like.

Hu-Man is the director of his/her own universal movie, because Hu-Man is structured as a literal duplicate carbon copy of everything that is in the universe. All material creation is built in a general pattern of duality. Soul and Body. Illusion vs. Reality.

Soul develops on the astral and etheric planes, but is inherently imbued with all the mental substance from the planes above. The soul is impregnated with spirit. As spirit is energetic, it is imperishable, infinite, everlasting, and eternal.

The flesh body is the clothing for the soul. The soul, once encapsulated in the flesh body, can develop the human attributes of personality. It cannot do this in the astral etheric body. Once a lifetime is lived in the flesh body—the soul experiencing life in matter—develops personality. When the material lifetime is over, the personality and its life's actions are retained and recorded for the soul in the Akashic Records, *The Book of Life*. These records are stored in the astral planes.

 The placement of the planetary bodies in the heavens at the time of the human birth and rebirth determines the energies and impulses the soul will experience in a coming lifetime yet to be lived. The soul, in the body, has the choice to determine what actions it will take. That which is celestially determined is merely potentiality for the soul. We have the freedom of choice to do God's will. Then we become free. This is how the soul reincarnates.

We are the unified field.
We are the Unity.
We are One.
We are love.
I AM love. This is everything.

I Am the theory of everything and so are you if you so choose to be.

Appendix 1: Book References

The Third Jesus by Deepak Chopra 2008
The Passover Plot by Dr. Hugh Schonfield 1965
Webster's New World Dictionary 1961
Life on the Other Side by Sylvia Brown 2000
The Everything Astrology Book by Trish MacGregor 1999
The Message Of The Stars by Max and Augusta Heindel 1927
The Aquarian Gospel of Jesus the Christ by Levi 1895
The Astrologers Handbook by Sakoian and Acker 1975
Planets In Aspect by Robert Peletier 1973
The Beatles circa 1968
The Transformation Of Man by Lewis Mumford 1930
The Secret Teachings Of Jesus by Lewis Spencer 1920
The Handbook To Higher Consciousness by Ken Keyes Jr. 1975
The Cosmic Code by Heinz Pagels 1982
Through Time Into Healing by Dr. Brian L. Weiss 1990
Bhagavad Gita A long time ago
The Reappearance of The Christ by Alice A. Bailey 1948
The Sacred Symbols Of Mu by James Churchward 1933
Edgar Cayce On The Dead Sea Scrolls 1970
Edgar Cayce On Reincarnation by Noel Langley 1970s
Life After Death-The burden Of Proof by Dr. Deepak Chopra 2007
Basic Psychology by Tracey Kendler 1963
The Lost Jesus Scroll by Elizabeth MacGregor 2007
Essential Judaism by George Robinson 2000
Cutting Through Spiritual Materialism - Chungpa Rimpoche 1975

Finite and Infinite Games - James Carce 1990s
The Physics Of Immortality by Dr. Frank Tipler 1995

Pope Arrested For Believing In Reincarnation

In 545 A.D., Roman Emperor Justinian forced the ruling cardinals to draft a papal decree stating that anyone who believes that souls come from God and return to God will be punished by death. History shows that the early Christian church Fathers believed in reincarnation and that souls journey back and forth (reincarnate) until they become One with God. In 250 A.D. the theologian Origen wrote of the pre-existence of the soul, that the soul's source was God and after lessons learned in multiple lifetimes on earth the soul can return to being One with God. In the 6th century Pope Vigilius and Emperor Justinian disagreed about the teachings of Origen being consistent with the teachings of Jesus so Justinian condemned all teachings on reincarnation. Pope Vigilius refused to sign the papal decree, was arrested and sentenced to prison. However, he escaped. To this day Christianity finds reincarnation anathema to their faith. This could not be farther from the truth. Hebrews 9:27 does not disprove reincarnation. Upon reading the entire chapter 9 one discovers the subject was about whether or not Jesus had to be sacrificed more than once.

Epilogue

In my past life as Jesus I was always consciously aware that the elements of creation were my thoughts, words and deeds. I knew that my thoughts would create my future life and that at the pre appointed time I would awaken, remember and recreate who I truly AM.

The words and deeds of Jesus created the indelible record that became encapsulated in the cellular memory that survived death to be re-remembered in the future lifetime as Bruce.

The patterns are constantly recreated lifetime after lifetime.

The "Goal of the Soul" is to wake up and remember that we are above all soul beings and not just human beings.

Then our words and deeds will reflect our thoughts of peace, love and goodwill to each other. True creation comes when we remember and recreate who we are......

Gods

www.ingramcontent.com/pod-product-compliance
Lightning Source LLC
LaVergne TN
LVHW051555070426
835507LV00021B/2591